Praise for

Love First

"McLaughlin's book is written for such a time as this! It is a clarion call for the church to reconnect to its most fundamental doctrine, the doctrine of love. He makes a convincing case that the doctrine of love could very well be the major doctrine of the church that has received the least amount of explicit attention dating all the way back to the ancient church creeds. *Love First* reminds the Christian community that its primary allegiance is to God and that the kingdom love ethic must guide Christian behavior in all areas of life including the world of racial brutality and political warfare! Instead of reading books that deal with the arts of war, seduction, and power, Christians would do well to read McLaughlin's *Love First*! This book provides profound insights into the art of love!"

—**Jerry Taylor,** Assistant Professor of Bible, Missions, and Ministry Abilene Christian University

"I can't imagine a topic that needs more attention than love: true, gritty, gospel-formed love. As McLaughlin says in *Love First*, there is plenty of hate, and it doesn't work. This wonderful book moves beyond slogans and logos. It is challenging, practical, and compelling."

—**Mike Cope,** Director of Ministry Outreach, Pepperdine University

"*Love First* takes us back to the core message of the Gospel of Jesus Christ. McLaughlin will inspire you to reprioritize your life and give you a renewed sense of vision for how you can be someone that is both transformed by a love from God, as well as becoming someone that then transmits that love to a world that so desperately needs it."

—**Daniel Hill,** author of *10:10: Life to the Fullest*

LOVE FIRST

LOVE FIRST

ENDING HATE BEFORE IT'S TOO LATE

DON MCLAUGHLIN

LOVE FIRST

Ending Hate Before It's Too Late

an imprint of Abilene Christian University Press

ISBN 978-0- 89112-474-0

Printed in the United States of America

Library of Congress Cataloging-in-Publication Data is on file at the Library of Congress, Washington DC.

Cover design by ThinkPen Design, LLC
Interior text design by Sandy Armstrong, Strong Design

Leafwood Publishers is an imprint of Abilene Christian University Press
ACU Box 29138
Abilene, Texas 79699

1-877-816-4455
www.leafwoodpublishers.com

17 18 19 20 21 22 / 7 6 5 4 3 2 1

For My Dad

Who left us a Love-First legacy

1931–2014

PREFACE

Love and hate. People treat these like two sides of the same coin . . . like light and dark or hot and cold. But the "thin line" between love and hate is as broad as the chasm between good and evil, life and death, Hitler and Mother Teresa. Opposites are often beneficial, but hate is of no benefit to love. *We do not need hate to appreciate love.* God does not need hate to make his love appealing. Hate will not be in heaven. Hate's time is running out.

But hate is wreaking havoc now, and we need to end hate before it's too late. Who would suggest the world needs more hate? How many more lives will we sacrifice to hate before we get serious about turning this around?

Hate has a long and tragic history in the human story, but only love is eternal. God is love. Hate emerged from our holy and sacred ability to choose who and what we would love, *or not*. Hate is not from God, but the freedom to choose one over the other is, and God has made his choice: "We love *because he first loved us*."

This is Love-First. We know what love is because of the choices God has made. His love is generous. His love is active. His love overcomes our resistance. His love takes our breath away. His love precedes everything we know about him or receive from him. Remember, "For God so loved the world that he gave . . ."

The church was birthed in love. Our existence is an expression of the perfect love of the Father, Son, and Holy Spirit. We are filled and sustained by God's love and *we are His love in the flesh*. When people encounter the church they experience God's love. But not everyone . . . and not always . . .

So why does the church hate?

This question plagues our mission. If the church wasn't born to love, the world wouldn't be on our case about our hating ways. People don't cuss at the desert when it's dry, nor do they scream at the ocean because it's wet. People learn to accept what's expected. But since the church is expected to love, the world rightly calls out our hypocrisy when we come across as hateful.

You might resist that last paragraph, so let me offer it a different way. I know *we want* people to see love in us, *we want* people to hear love from us, and *we want* people to experience love through us, but we've lost our mirror. We don't see ourselves as the world sees us. We don't hear ourselves the way they do, nor do we sense that our words and deeds are that far from the loving message of God.

I wrote this book to challenge this assumption. This book is meant to be a mirror for me and for you. The church is at a crossroads that even secular historians recognize. This moment in history is critical to our future. We must reclaim the Love-First life that God shares with us, and end hate before it's too late.

My intent is to offer a perspective on where we are, how we got here, and how to fully live into the Love-First vision God has for his world.

Thank you for joining me on this quest to end hate before it's too late.

Don McLaughlin

2017

CONTENTS

Introduction—Why Love-First Matters 13

Part 1
The Love/Hate Crisis

1 A Sick Church in a Sick World 23
2 Diagnosis and Healing 39

Part 2
The Divine Love Intervention

3 Love-less Creeds 55
4 The Right Kind of Love 69
5 God-Shaped Love 81
6 The Love-First Reformation 89

Part 3
The Love-First Revolution

7 The Corinthian Conditions 101
8 Love Is Patient 109
9 Love Is Kind 119
10 Love Is Not Envious 133
11 Love Is Not Boastful or Proud 147
12 Love Is Not Rude 159
13 Love Is Not Self-Seeking 167
14 Love Is Not Easily Angered 177

15 Love Keeps No Record of Wrongs 187
16 Love Does Not Delight in Injustice 197

Part 4
Love First, Always, and Never

17 In the World, But Not of the World 211
18 Love Always Protects 223
19 Love Always Trusts 231
20 Love Never Gives Up 239
21 Love Always Hopes 245
22 Love Always Endures 257
23 Our Love-*less* Past 261
24 Love Never Disappears 269

Conclusion—One Thing Remains 281
Endnotes 285

Introduction

WHY LOVE-FIRST MATTERS

I APOLOGIZE. I was wrong. I need a do-over.

I've been a pastor for thirty-five years. I have gone to school a lot. I talk too much. I love God. I love people. I love being a son, sibling, father, grandfather, neighbor, and friend. I love my church and my city. I'm an unapologetic follower of Jesus Christ, and I believe he is right about everything.

But *I am not right about everything*, and I really blew it on this one, so I need to just get it out in the open so that I can humbly repent. God's love is *not* unconditional.

Yes. You read that correctly. It is not a misprint or misspelling. The love of God is *conditional*. The kind of love Christians are supposed to give is conditional. The love God intends for grandparents, parents, spouses, and your BFF is conditional. The church is called to an extreme, conditional love.

I know, I know. This can't be so! Everyone knows God's love is unconditional, and most of us have beautiful stories of love in our lives that have been filed under "Unconditional Love." I preached it, and I encouraged everyone I met to believe it. *But I was wrong.* There may be such a thing as unconditional love, but it is not the love of God, and it is not the love the world needs.

Now, either you're at least moderately interested in the direction this is headed, or you're ready to toss this book in the trash. Please hang with me long enough for me to make my case. I'm trying to repent here . . . so think of reading this book as a way to help me make things right.

I now believe unconditional love is our problem, but obviously I didn't always think this way. If your experience and mine overlap at all, my guess is that the "unconditional" love of God has been imprinted on your soul like a tattoo. Unhooking from this treasured, hallowed thought is not going to be easy. The idea of God's unconditional love (as I understood it) has given me the hope and strength I needed to face my greatest fears, failures, and frustrations. I don't know how I would have made it this far without the unconditional love of God. (Can you relate?)

But guess what: We did make it this far without the unconditional love of God, because there is no such thing!

If what I've shared so far seems as disorienting to you as it first did to me, consider Joan and Amy. They sat across from me in my office with bloodshot eyes and streaked makeup. Joan was there because her marriage had exploded. Amy was there because she cared. An email from Joan had given me the basics:

Married twenty years to her high school sweetheart.

Devastated by revelations of his now-public affair.

Packed his stuff and moved in with his girlfriend.

No remorse.

Her friend had helped her set up a session with a counselor, but she wanted to stop by for prayer with her pastor on the way to that appointment.

"Do you want to pray *with* me, or would you like me to pray *for* you?" I asked.

Her reply still stings, "You will have to pray for me . . . I just feel dead."

Joan is one of the countless "living dead" I've encountered in decades of pastoral ministry, people with a zest for life who have been reduced to emotional zombies when love has been replaced with betrayal, abandonment, or abuse. And hurts like this are not limited to women, or only to marriage. One of my mentors, who spent a lifetime healing from an abusive father, shared with me, "Life without love is known by another name: death." Anyone who has loved hard and been betrayed knows this death. But as much as we want to give up on love, we really don't. Bad love can cut so deep we want to die. But no matter how much it hurts, we cannot extinguish the longing for *good* love.

I have been entranced with the love of God since he first captured my heart. I believed from the start that God's love could and would heal our broken relationships and transform our world. But that world seems to have changed—to something so much worse. Who would have thought even twenty years ago that ruthless beheadings by terrorists would be posted online so that a nine-year-old could click on it? It's unimaginable that murderous attacks at malls, coffee shops, elementary schools, and family-filled city squares would be the norm. Slavery is still grinding up the lives of children, and profit from sex trafficking is second only to the illegal drug trade worldwide. Why is the human race so inhuman?

I am guessing that both you and I long for real solutions to these and countless more senseless tragedies. I am still convinced that God's love is the answer. This conviction drives me to seek ways to expand the tangible impact of God's love into every arena of my life.

At first I believed that the problem was the gap between the *conditional* love humans offer each other and the *unconditional* love offered by God. So, in the summer of 2013, I set out on a fresh study of the Bible to better understand and share the unconditional love of God. Not far into my study I began to get frustrated. I had expected to find the unconditional love of God on every page, but I found myself asking, "Where is it? Where is this *un*conditional love of God that I've heard about all my life?" Maybe I just wasn't studying deep enough. I decided to launch a fresh study in Genesis and not quit until I arrived safely in Revelation with a stack of scriptures confirming the tried and true doctrine of the *un*conditional love of God. But as I flipped to the final page of God's Book of Love, my page was blank. I had not recorded even one verse documenting His *un*conditional love. I was frustrated, embarrassed, and confused. How had I preached this so boldly and affirmed it so blindly? Two journal entries bookmark my study:

> **Journal Entry: August 4, 2013**
> "We love because he first loved us" (1 John 4:19). God sent Jesus because he loved the world. But Jesus is the Lamb slain *before* the foundation of the world (1 Pet. 1:20; Rev. 13:8). This has to mean that God loved us before he created us. He loved first, and everything—*everything*—came after love. Love is who God is and what God does ahead of everything else. This is the love to which he is calling me: Love First.

> **Journal Entry: July 4, 2016**
> God's love is always conditional, and that is what makes it perfect. I must abandon my unconditional love if I want to love like him. Lord, give me the strength and courage necessary to live your divinely conditioned love.

This book is the outcome of three years of study that turned up nothing and yet revealed everything. These two journal entries emerged from my determination to prove one thing but my willingness to discover another. Love-First is a revolutionary movement that empowers engagement, heals wounds, creates intimacy, ends oppression, liberates the enslaved, and binds together our frayed families, churches, neighborhoods, and nation.

Why Love-First Matters

Let's get real: Hate is oozing out of the pores and sores of humanity. People are spewing hate at the slightest provocation. Reacting to criticism with hateful insults has been normalized from politicians to preachers, from grandmas in line at Walmart to middle-school bullies on social media. And it is killing us. We must end hate before it's too late. But the answer has to be tangible and doable.

The Love-First revolution is *the* answer. It is God's answer, but we intuitively know it is our answer as well. Hate doesn't work, even when we are wounded, hurt, or so mad we could bite a nail in half. Hate is our frustrated response to bad love, so not just any love will do, or the cycle of bad love birthing hate will continue to spiral out of control. In this book I am advocating a love that is rooted in God and is conditioned by his divine heart.

Here are my three commitments in this book:

1. The information, experiences, and stories in this book will make your life better. That is not a boast. I just want to set a clear expectation for how important and effective this study can be for you.
2. I will not waste your time. I will not play around, nor will I skip over the hard stuff. I promise to share with empathy but with candor.
3. Every relationship in your life will be upgraded as you put this kind of love into practice.

Here are the three promises I can't make:

1. I cannot promise that you will like or agree with everything in this book. All I ask is that when you

disagree, don't be lazy. Check stuff out. Do your research, and develop informed discernment.

2. I cannot make you easy to get along with. If you are immature, stubborn, or throw a fit when people confront you, then what I share here will still help, but not without some tough moments. All I ask is that you give your best. If you get stuck, get with someone else and tell them how important it is for you to grow up in love. Let them know that you need their help, even if that means they need to tell you stuff you haven't handled well in the past.
3. I cannot make anyone love you. If you love someone and they are not loving you the way you wish they would, give them a copy of this book. It will improve their love if they put it into practice, but they may end up loving someone else the way you wish they'd love you. Even if that did happen, this book will help you love them better, and it will prepare you to love and be loved by someone else.

Three things you need to maximize this experience:

1. You need this book and some way to record your "aha" moments.
2. You need a friend or small group who will go through it with you.
3. You need to put things into practice as you read them, and then keep refining each step as you go.

This book isn't for everyone who needs it. It is only for those who want it. I grew up in construction. We put in all the foundational elements below ground so that successful building could take place above ground. I am a big believer in doing the foundational work we need in order to achieve the success we want.

So Here Is the Plan

We will go through this study in four sections, each building on the previous one.

- The Love/Hate Crisis—Let's identify why something as promising as love is the source of so much pain. Then we will diagnose some of our love wounds and how to heal them.
- The Divine Love Intervention—What does Jesus bring to love that is fundamentally unique and makes ending hate a reachable goal?
- The Love-First Revolution—I believe the secret to God's divine love is in the conditions he has set. When lived with enthusiasm and commitment, these conditions will absolutely transform (and upgrade) every relationship in your life. Led by Scripture, let's let God tell us *what love is, and what love is not.*
- Love First, Always, and Never—Our response to cultural shifts and challenges has not always reflected God's kind of love. If we love as he loves, what qualities must our love always reflect, and never reflect?

Throughout this book, I will weave in stories of the church, our communities, national and international events, and our individual lives.[1] Each one of these entities is important because they interact with and are interdependent on each other. I am going to drill down into Scripture. I know this may or may not be appealing to all, so I just ask that you hang with me. You do not have to have a particular belief in the Bible in order to benefit profoundly from the wisdom you will discover there.

Am I crazy for writing a book on love, and crazier still for assuming you would read it? Aren't there already ten thousand books on love? Yes. But I don't think the abundance of books has equated to an abundance of love.

While in grad school, I took a class taught by Archbishop Desmond Tutu. He was coming off the taxing task of leading the Truth and Reconciliation Commission in South Africa. The theme of God's love provided the context for every lesson. One afternoon he brought our class a message I will never forget. "I hear that some of you are grumbling that I need to move on from talking about the love of God," the good bishop started off. Then he explained, "The stall in progress is not my fault; if you would get it, I would move on." This book is my commitment to "getting it."

Part 1

THE LOVE/ HATE CRISIS

A SICK CHURCH IN A SICK WORLD

Few health crises have rocked the world as totally as the African outbreak of Ebola, a disease virtually unknown before it hit our headlines. The following story appeared in Reuters on June 27, 2014:

> **Were Good Doctors Making People Sick?**
> An Ebola patient whose family forcefully removed her from a hospital to take her to a traditional healer has died. A nationwide hunt was sparked for the patient after she was removed from the King Harman hospital in Sierra Leone's capital Freetown. Amadu Sisi, a senior doctor at the hospital, said police found her in the house of a healer. Her family refused to hand her over and a struggle ensued with police, who finally retrieved her and sent her to a hospital, he said. "She died in the ambulance on the way to another hospital," Sisi added. Health officials say fear and mistrust of health

> workers in Sierra Leone, where many have more faith in traditional medicine, are hindering efforts to contain an Ebola outbreak which has killed more than 450 people in the country. . . . A 33-year-old American doctor working for relief organization Samaritan's Purse in Liberia tested positive for the disease on Saturday.

As the Ebola crisis unfolded, it would emerge that the American doctor in that news account was Kent Brantley, nephew of my co-pastor, Ken Snell. I had met Kent and his family in Indianapolis when he was a boy. Now he was international news, the face of medical heroism, and now infected with that dreaded, deadly disease. After his miraculous healing and recovery at Emory University Hospital in Atlanta, Kent came to our church one Sunday morning to share his story.

He noted that generations of superstition, complicated by mistrust of health workers, led many to believe people were contracting Ebola *at the hospital*. This led to a family forcibly entering the clinic to "rescue" their family member, only later to watch her die. Protesters gathered outside hospitals and clinics, clashing with police and threatening to burn down buildings and remove the patients.

Kent's family has a history of wrapping the love of Jesus in the gift of medical care. He and his wife moved their family to Liberia to serve. Being the *Time Magazine* Person of the Year was the furthest thing from his mind. When their story was published in 2015, the book was titled, *Called for Life: How Loving Our Neighbor Led Us into the Heart of the Ebola Epidemic*. The whole journey was about love. But the very people they came to help believed Dr. Brantley and his co-workers were the problem. What a tragic twist in an already terrible situation.

Kent's story resonates with my reason for writing this book. I believe the crisis of our time is that those commissioned by Christ to bring healing to the world often are seen as the problem, not the solution. This may be the most serious crisis Christians face today. *Is there a greater crisis than a problem masquerading as a solution, an illness disguised as a cure?*

Is the World Sick of a Sick Church?

The church's falling favorability rating has been documented for more than four decades. Some fascinating research revealed that church people give themselves a consistently higher rating than the world does. Some even suggest that any lack of popular favor is witness to the church's counter-cultural message of holiness and truth. In essence, they say *we are so holy the world hates us.* But this doesn't seem to bear the weight of research. Most who diss the church cite its unloving and judgmental disposition, not its fundamental doctrines. In fact, most who experience the judgmentalism of the church do not see this as an indication of our holiness!

The doctors and medical providers in West Africa worked tirelessly to win the trust of those who desperately needed them. Could the church take a chapter out of their book? These dedicated medical personnel couldn't serve the sick unless they changed how the sick perceived them. As painful as it is to confess, the church also has a credibility problem, and we must face it to fix it. I believe we can diagnose and heal our disconnectedness with the world, but to do so effectively, we must view our symptoms through their eyes. This exercise is essential for the church to regain a place of trust and healing in the marketplace.

Symptoms of a Sick Church

Let's begin with the most noticeable symptoms first and then work toward the more difficult. I promised in the introduction to be candid, even if it makes us feel uneasy or frustrated. It is not my mission to frustrate anyone, but we can't get well if we don't acknowledge that we are sick!

Symptom One: The Best People Fit in with Me

The church has the reputation of believing we are better than everyone else—that you have to be a "certain kind of person" to fit in with us.

Consider my friend Cynthia. Here is the love deposit she left on my Facebook page: "I love, love, love our church!" I reached out to her with a private message and asked her to tell me more about why she was *really* feeling the love. She said, "I feel so at home. I'm accepted, respected, and loved at North Atlanta. Look, I'm a single, black professional woman making my way back from two years of hell in cocaine addiction. I don't know where else I could have fit in."

Although to me Cynthia is simply my sister in Christ, her *self-description* is full of demographic markers. She's an African-American, unmarried female, who is both a corporate professional and a recovering addict. Cynthia is not an anomaly in our church but that means *our church is an anomaly* in American Christianity. A LifeWay Research poll showed in 2015 that 86 percent of churches in the United States are ethnically homogenous. In response to these findings, former executive director of LifeWay Research, Dr. Ed Stetzer notes, "Surprisingly, most churchgoers are content with the ethnic status quo in their churches. In a world where our culture is increasingly diverse, and many pastors are talking about diversity, it appears most people are happy where they are—and *with* who they are."

Bryan Loritts, lead pastor at Abundant Life Christian Fellowship, Mountain View, California, follows Stetzer's observation with his own: "There remains little to no desire to change when it comes to issues of diversity. The recent statistics unearthed by the LifeWay Research team serve, on a much deeper level, as a stethoscope, allowing us to hear the rhythms of our hearts. Rhythms that I believe are out of step with the gospel. That's the tragic takeaway."[1]

As of this writing, the U.S. population is nearing three hundred twenty-five million, positioning us as the third largest nation in the world behind China and India. We make up only 4.4 percent of the world's population. There are other industrialized countries with greater percentages of ethnic diversity, but none with our raw numbers. Over 80 percent of our population lives in large, urban/metro centers.

Especially in our cities, we shop, work, play, and go to school with people who are different. I believe that most Americans want to come across as informed, just, and ethical people, but many harbor deeply polarizing internal beliefs and preferences that serve to exclude others. These beliefs and preferences are manifested in what Chester M. Pierce termed "microaggression." Casual insults, slights, and dismissals may amount to a degradation and marginalizing of people. Microaggressions are sweeping statements that express an existing negative view of a particular gender, ethnicity, or socio-economic group. For example, someone suggests in the lunchroom at work that "the illegals are nothing but criminals and rapists," or "it's the gays who are destroying the morals of our great country." And though some will nod in agreement, there are others who sit silently in dissent. They know these opinions are neither verifiable nor based in any factual study, but they also don't want lunch to turn into an argument. The person making the comment usually sees nothing wrong with what they said. In fact, they might believe they had a responsibility to stand up for what they think is right, though they do not recognize the damage to others caused by their negative categorical characterizations. And yes . . . there are casualties.

In an article titled, "The Ugly in Christianity," Hillary Ferguson notes,

> I proudly called myself a Christian. Now I shy away from the term. I avoid discussions about it because I

have family members I love so much who are still part of the Church. But, I will never again be one of them. And I'll tell you why: when I was 18, a freshman in college, on the cusp of adulthood, already questioning my faith and whether or not I even believed in organized religion, a woman stood up in a Wednesday Bible class and said, "Praise the Lord! Ted Kennedy is dead!" I sat there slack-jawed, shocked and disgusted, and the dimming light to my already fragile faith flickered out as everybody in the room—even an elder—laughed.

They laughed and laughed, and the woman said, "If I could, I'd go dance on his grave." She did a little jig and turned around with her hands in the air and again, once again, there was more laughter. Louder laughter. I wish I could say that was an isolated event. But things like that happened often. They happened and nobody stopped them, and judging by Facebook comments, I'm pretty sure they probably continue today.

The truth is, that kind of attitude cannot coexist with God in any form. And I refuse to be a part of any organization that would affiliate with that kind of rhetoric. Perhaps that one room doesn't define the Church of Christ as a whole, but I've been to enough of them, met enough of the members, to know that the people who wouldn't have laughed are the outliers. And for every one outlier Church of Christ member I've met, I've encountered nine others who would dance on a dead man's grave, or laugh at it.

I loved that Church dearly, I truly did. But at some point, *I learned that the love of the Church only extended to the end of its borders, to the end of the doors* [emphasis added]. Outside those doors, there was very little love to give. I felt betrayed by their laughter, by their dirty

> words. I felt disheartened, and I was turned away from God—most likely never to return. If that was an example of God's love, I'd rather seek love elsewhere.[2]

My heart breaks *for* Hillary, but first it breaks *with* her. I am a preaching minister in a Church of Christ. As I read the lines she wrote, and the ones she didn't, I wanted to say, "Hillary, please come and stay with us in Atlanta . . . Come to church with us . . . Experience the love God has been growing in this place." But then reality humbled me. I would have to make sure to steer her away from those who speak like the very people she described. I still want her to come and experience the amazing love I'm immersed in through our church, but I would have to first say, "Hillary, we are sick too, but we want to get well!" Eighteen-year-old Hillary didn't fit in because she couldn't catch even a hint of hope that Christians would honor the humanity of others, displaying the love of Christ even in disagreement.

Symptom Two: The Smartest People Think Like Me

The conversations in our church hallways, small groups, and after-worship lunches reveal the thinking of a church.

In his book, *Renovation of the Heart*, Dallas Willard notes (and I paraphrase him here) that our inner self has been formed by the world, but it must be transformed by the Spirit of God. Paul urges this "renewal of the mind" so that we may know God's perfect and pleasing will (Rom. 12:1–2). How good is our thinking? Does it go through a renewal process that holds it up to the perfect will of God for habitual refinement?

The racial divisions in our world are present in our churches, and this is a relevant test case for examining the health of our thinking. Over the past few years as the African-American community has brought focused attention to race-related inequities in our policing, prosecution, and prison institutions, many white

Christians have closed their ears and hearts. Instead of offering empathy, they shouted back and quoted statistics of black-on-black crime, as if black-on-black crime is responsible for white-on-black racism. This has painted a fresh coat of racism on the church. The more that white Christians have repeated these ideas to each other over social media and in face-to-face social gatherings, the more we have believed our thinking was correct.

We are what we think. Whatever is stored in our minds will come out in our words and actions. So if we assume our assessment of others is fully informed and completely correct, we will act in accordance with these notions.

Our Scriptures offer a huge advantage for those who desire clear-minded thinking. In them we are taught how to listen, learn, and discern. Along with teaching us the processes and attitudes required for good thinking, Scripture also outlines the rewards that attend those who energetically pursue godly wisdom.

For example, love that humbly listens to others with empathy has an enormous peacemaking influence, thus expanding the possibility for unity through love. Those equipped with the divine mind can construct love and deconstruct systems of hate (Jas. 3:13–18). Those who plant peace harvest harmony. But it proves to be easier to teach a Sunday school class about humility, peace, and wisdom than it is to actually be humble, peaceful, and wise. As Hillary Ferguson so painfully pointed out, we have normalized combative reaction rather than thoughtfulness. Those watching us are both inside and outside the church walls.

We have been seduced into the mire of false dichotomies, seeing irreconcilable points of view in nearly every religious and political discussion. In *The Mosaic of Christian Belief*, conservative Christian author and professor of theology at Baylor University, Roger Olson, offers this observation: "Perhaps many of the doctrinal divisions that have arisen are due to unnecessary bifurcations—false alternatives. *Either/or thinking becomes a habit*. People fail to look for combinations, the truth in both sides. What if instead . . . God's people looked long and hard for the truth in seemingly irreconcilable but equally biblically supported beliefs and doctrines?"[3] Could it be that we place a higher value on individual expression than on individuals? Many confessing Christians lack the self-discipline necessary to give facts a fighting chance to influence our thinking. Along with this lack of passion for meaningful information, we also lack both the maturity for wisdom and the courage for truth.

Could it be that we place a higher value on individual expression than on individuals?

Our overly individualistic culture in the West is partly to blame for how we think. We are addicted to self-expression, and we have an inflated estimation of the value of our thinking. We say much, but without critical thinking or research. Then we feel the need to defend our statements or suffer embarrassment. A friend of mine who preaches for a church nearby refreshingly confessed, "I've never held an opinion I didn't *think* was right, but with age and reflection I've learned that all were either *incomplete* or *incorrect* in some way." Opposite this preacher's transparency are the church leaders who accuse anyone who thinks differently from them of being "intellectually dishonest." Their assumption is, "When you believe differently than me, it is both a mental and moral mark on your character. You have to think like me to be both right *and* good." This is sick thinking!

Symptom Three: The Safest People Fear What I Fear

The summer of 2016. Racial tension was everywhere. Names like Alton Sterling, Philando Castile, and Micah Johnson flooded newsfeeds and social media. Videos went viral, anger boiled over, officers walking with peaceful protesters were gunned down in Dallas. People wanted this problem fixed. We needed solutions, and it felt like the church could and should help, but there wasn't a great interest. Right after 9/11, churches were filled to overflowing, but less than two decades later, Twitter and Facebook played a greater role than the church in addressing pain, anger, frustration, and division.

Through that long summer, police chiefs, pundits, and politicians all weighed in on the problem. Some of the dialogue was helpful; much was ugly, accusatory, bombastic, and dangerous. Some blamed our first black president for the rise in racism in our country. Others indicted President-elect Donald Trump for inciting violence with his inflammatory remarks. The Black Lives Matter movement was venerated by some and vilified by others. Many were caught in a painful dilemma between feeling a deep respect for the police while processing the mounting and undeniable evidence of racial inequities in our law enforcement institutions.

Stark ironies then emerged: Dallas Police Chief David Brown and Charlotte-Mecklenburg Police Chief Kerr Putney, both black men in blue uniforms, spoke of the painful realities our country had to face. They spoke with fierce loyalty and love for their officers in blue, but they also used their unique position to speak bluntly to the decades of racist policing that had indelibly marked both men from their earliest memories. *These were law enforcement officers talking about fearing law enforcement officers.* These dedicated officers articulated for us a dual perspective that needs to be heard, but many on either side have been unwilling to listen to anyone who stretched their preconceived opinions. Fear has us in a death grip.

The church should be comforting when the world is hurting—fearless when the world is fearful. The Sunday following the tragedies in Baton Rouge, Minneapolis, and Dallas, we offered prayer meetings, preaching, blogs, and posts . . . but the nation wasn't listening. Anyone with a Twitter account owned this conversation, and *not* the preachers, pastors, and priests. Why? The answer is both complicated and simple. The complexity is in the social makeup and history of religious movements in America. The burdensome reality is that churches are moved more by fear than by love. In a tragic twist of Scripture, *perfect fear has cast out love* from most of our churches, and this keeps us on edge. Rather than being peacemakers, we build walls and spread suspicion.

In the wake of the shootings in Minneapolis, Baton Rouge, and Dallas, I posted some messages online encouraging Christians to create safe spaces where people could share their hurts, anger, and opinions without fear of putdowns or retaliation. One man wrote back, "How does that help? If you give these *animals* any encouragement, they will destroy the country, and don't think you will be safe." Yes, that is a direct response when I encouraged Christians to be peacemakers. Some call this "venting." God uses a different word: "Sin."

Is the church willing to serve once again as an outlier to this culture of fear, as a lighthouse of rest in a sea of rage? To do so will require reframing what it means to be a servant of Christ on behalf of the world.

Symptom Four: The Good People Are Good Like Me

In the summer of 2016, many Christians took a stand in solidarity with the police (Blue Lives Matter) in opposition to the Black Lives Matter movement. Ironically, many of these same Christians voiced raving reviews of Chief Brown who praised the Black Lives Matter marchers in Dallas for their non-violent, peaceful protest. He understood that not everyone in a movement has the same motives or even the same understanding of the purpose of the movement.

He spoke personally of the racism he has experienced all his life. He publicly expressed empathy and support for the marchers. But while many Christians gushed over Chief Brown, they *comprehensively* condemned the Black Lives Matter movement. How are we to understand the acceptance of him as a policeman but the rejection of his experiences as a black citizen? Evidently, many liked the "blue half" of this black man but could not detect the inherent racism in this dissection of Chief Brown. They assigned good to a black man because being a policeman elevated his standing. This is racism, and racism is sin. Observers outside the church saw this as hypocritical. They wondered how you could have such high respect for Chief Brown and then *completely disregard his thoughts* about what happened in his city or what was happening around our country regarding the black community and policing. This is hard to write and hard to read. I am a white man who must seriously examine my implicit biases.

As a way to encourage more open and honest dialogue concerning race and faith, I chose to be a collaborator and signer of a letter published nationally to encourage churches to hear the pains being articulated by the black community. Some of my friends wanted to know if I agreed with everything in the letter. I replied, "I agree with about ninety percent, and the ten percent I don't agree with represents experiences that are different from my own. Had I walked life in their shoes, I might see it exactly as they wrote it."

I know many Christians who allow their opinions of others to be shaped more by their favorite news network than by the Good News.

The expectation of unblemished goodness or complete agreement is a false prerequisite for love, support, or respect. Scripture specifically says that "there is no one who does good, *not even one*" (Rom. 3:12). This does not mean that humans never do good, but that not one of us can claim personal righteousness on our own merits. God commands compassion and respect for others, including those who are not *totally* good, and those we do not agree with. While we may opt to offer meaningful critique and non-violent resistance when we believe others are oppressive and unjust, still Christ-followers must seriously challenge the notion that our political, cultural, and religious views are the gold standard for what is good and right in the world. I know many Christians who allow their opinions of others to be shaped more by their favorite news network than by the Good News. Their willingness to see good in others is predicated on political agreement rather than on our priceless atonement.

Consider the story told by the apostle John about Jesus meeting Nathanael. When he learned that Jesus was from Nazareth, Nathanael asked, "Can anything good come out of Nazareth?" (John 1:43–51). His upbringing had conditioned him to believe that anything or anyone from Nazareth was bad, *not good.* But Nathanael was wrong about who might be right. If the people around us must somehow conform to our standards of thought, belief, opinion, or behavior before we can benevolently engage with them and see the possibility of good in them, we are not Christian in word or deed.

On June 15, 2015, a white policeman in Austin, Texas, explained to a twenty-six-year-old black school teacher that many people are afraid of black people because African-Americans have "violent tendencies." This case received international attention, because the scene of the officer body-slamming her to the pavement during the traffic stop was caught on video and uploaded to the Internet. The policeman's actions seemed to suggest that a tendency toward violence might not be a skin-color issue. While being arrested, Breaion King, who was pursuing her master's degree at Texas State University, asked the officer to consider the racism in his observation, but he was quick to challenge her by asking if racism "goes both ways."

My motivation for bringing up this case is not to push you to decide if the one was more at fault than the other, or if a black, female school teacher deserves more support than a white, male police officer. I am more interested in how people *form their perceptions* of good or evil. For some, the color of skin is a basic way to assign good or evil, violence or peace. Some in law enforcement were slow to judge the physical altercation between the officer and Ms. King, but they were quick to note that the officer's *categorical equating of violence to skin color is neither professional nor supported by crime statistics*. And since I am a white male, if I subscribe to the officer's false supposition, I will have to recategorize all the abuse and violence committed every hour of every day by people *with my level of melanin*!

Assessing the potential for violence according to skin color, gender, immigration status, or religion does not bear up under the most elementary rigors of research. Ruby Bridges-Hall was speaking to our church in Atlanta when she explained: "The problem is not white, black, or brown. It is a problem of good and evil. When Dylan Roof, a white man, sits for an hour in a prayer meeting, and then stands up and shoots the very people who welcomed him, that is evil. But the person who murdered my son was the same color as my son. The issue was not skin color . . . it was good and evil."

Can We Help to Heal the World?

The four symptoms of spiritual illness we have just looked at point to one frightening diagnosis: We are sick! But the more important question is "What next?" If you remember Dr. Brantley's miraculous recovery from the deadly Ebola virus, it included bringing him from Liberia to Emory Hospital in Atlanta, Georgia. Some public figures vehemently objected to his return, making the case that he got sick over there and should stay over there, even if it killed him. It seemed unconscionable to most Americans that we would shut out one of our own citizens when he needed us most, but the fear of the virus was real. Officials and citizens summoned their courage and compassion and brought Kent home. I remember the tension-mixed-with-hope in Atlanta as we watched hospital workers in hazmat suits helping Kent from the back of the ambulance. Even if he didn't survive, we knew that bringing him in was right, and shutting him out was wrong. Kent's recovery clarified that building bridges brings healing while erecting walls makes us sick. Rather than carriers of the disease of hate, the church is called to be couriers of the cure of love.

As he spoke to our church family in Atlanta some months after his recovery, Kent made it crystal clear that it was the love of God that took him and his family to Liberia. He could have left when the Ebola crisis hit, but he was there for healing, and the love that took him there kept him there when his own life was in danger. His confession of faith in Christ was more than a personal hope in salvation; rather, it was a transformation of how Kent saw the world. When the people around him thought he was part of the problem, his love and sacrifice made it clear that he could be trusted to help them heal. His recovery was for them as much as it was for himself.

When the church realizes its need for healing, it becomes a place of healing for the world.

Love-First Reflections

- List the four symptoms that diagnose our sickness from Chapter One. Put an asterisk beside the symptoms you most recognize in yourself.

1. ______________________________
2. ______________________________
3. ______________________________
4. ______________________________

- Why is it important to see our symptoms not just through our own eyes but also through the eyes of the world?

- What are some of the negative outcomes when our "willingness to see good in others is predicated on political agreement rather than our priceless atonement?"

- Read James 3:13–18 and then complete the two columns below by listing attributes of each kind of wisdom you discover in the text.

Wisdom from Above	Wisdom Not from Above

DIAGNOSIS AND HEALING

The followers of Christ are rightly expected to be the absolute best at expressing his compassion. This expectation is enhanced by the way we describe the love of the church. So when we do not deliver on empathy, sympathy, and compassion, the world feels a deep sense of betrayal. But I cannot, and will not, accept that the church of Jesus will be remembered like Judas.

The World Is Waiting for a Healthy Church

The last chapter may have sounded like an unfair critique of the church. You may have wanted to shoot me, or at least to shoot me an email telling me of the wonderful things your church is doing. I want to assure you that I love the church and I'm ecstatic when I see the gospel bringing life, love, and liberation to millions around the world. But we cannot ignore trends, and we must not allow exceptions to mask the greater problem. The church, especially in the Global North, is in a titanic battle for the hearts of the last two generations who, like Hillary Ferguson, have decided to look elsewhere for the love they so desperately need. If we are not honest about the challenges we face, the world will simply move on without us.

Take in the prophetic words Dr. Martin Luther King Jr. delivered on December 18, 1963. While reflecting on the entrenched racism in American churches, he noted that the eleven o'clock hour on Sunday morning was the most segregated hour in America. But he further clarified the real crisis:

> Nobody of honesty can overlook this. Now, I'm sure that if the church had taken a stronger stand all along, we wouldn't have many of the problems that we have. The first way that the church can repent, the first way that it can move out into the arena of social reform is to remove the yoke of segregation from its own body. Now, I'm not saying that society must sit down and wait on a spiritual and moribund church as we've so often seen. I think it should have started in the church, but since it didn't start in the church, our society needed to move on.

This is hard to hear, but not hopeless. King did say that if the church does its part, many of the problems we face can be healed. We have a role, and by the grace of God and the power of the Spirit we can transform our space and place in society. But King also noted that this begins with repentance . . . an inner healing of the body of Christ.

The Healing Healer

Psychologist Carl Jung created a term, Wounded Healer, to capture the idea that personal wounds compel the analyst to treat the patient. Henri Nouwen used this term to title his classic work, *The Wounded Healer*. It is precisely in our woundedness and brokenness, Nouwen asserts, that we find ways to connect meaningfully with others for their healing. I want to suggest further that when the church is consciously attentive to healing its own woundedness, we are uniquely repositioned to offer meaningful healing to the world around us, both locally and globally.

Pope Francis offers a stunning example. He took office amid scandal. Acrimony described the relationships of the church's most powerful leaders. But Francis would not be doing religion as usual. One memorable moment came on March 28, 2013, when the world was treated to a picture of the pontiff on his knees, washing and kissing the feet of twelve prisoners in the Casal del Marmo jail on Rome's outskirts. The prisoners who received his gentle and compassionate touch included two Muslim women. This was unprecedented.

While the traditionalists seethed at Francis's apparent trivialization of convention, the world was entranced by this simple scene of authentic service. His humility was both inspiring and endearing. Who would have thought that people all around the world, including millennials and non-Catholics, would give Francis the highest approval rating of any international leader, religious or political?

In his first Holy Thursday Mass after being elected pope of the 1.2 billion-member Catholic Church, Francis charted a clear course: "We need to go out, then . . . to the outskirts where there is suffering, bloodshed, blindness that longs for sight, and prisoners in thrall to many evil masters."[1] Francis changed the face of his church without changing any foundational doctrine, and the world took notice. In a similar tone, I remember early in my ministry when a seasoned preacher shared, "I have not changed very many of my fundamental beliefs since I was a teenager, but I have changed the attitude with which I hold those beliefs."

My inspiration for challenging and encouraging the church to heal and live vibrantly in its calling in the world is rooted in my belief that a church that is healing from its own wounds can be a healing church among the wounded in our world.

A Willing Church

During the summer of 2016, Orpheus Heyward, senior minister for the West End Church of Christ in Atlanta, Georgia, hosted a unity meeting to bring the community together for a real conversation. He invited members of the police force, Black Lives Matter, Urban League of Greater Atlanta, and the NAACP, along with city officials, police training consultants, community activists, and clergy. Heyward's leadership was appreciated by all; the meeting was open, and people were free to speak bold truth. People listened to each other. The goal was not to manipulate outcomes but to develop relationships—to humanize the issues we were facing.

As I sat in the audience, I was encouraged and discouraged at the same time. I was one of less than a dozen white Christians among six hundred black brothers and sisters. I knew that many white Christians would not have been comfortable in such an open conversation where institutional power was confronted and held accountable. Emotion came through proclamation. Evocative questions were intentionally posed to the panel, and the audience made its voice heard. Most white churches are not equipped to welcome such full expressions of our humanity.

As the three-hour gathering too quickly moved toward its conclusion, Heyward called some pastors together to add Spirit truth to the conversation. But while some of the community activists and leaders stayed for the clergy panel, others left. As I saw them leave, my heart sank, but my respect for them did not. I knew why some of them left. The church has not been part of the solution; instead, it often has been the problem. Because of their experience, had they stayed and listened to the voice of the church, they assumed it would have only reopened old wounds. Much as Dr. King prophesied, they waited for the church too long, and finally they decided they had to move on without her. Of course, I wish they could have heard the amazing spiritual and practical insights delivered by my fellow pastors. I would have loved to further the dialogue with the leaders who left us that evening. But the church is reaping what it has sown. This is our present crisis.

Small Steps toward Sustainable Healing

I believe that small, meaningful, sustainable shifts in our attitudes, behaviors, and words will not only transform us, but will reposition the church to be trusted as a place for healing and a true partner in solving the great challenges that face us. But what does it look like if a church, or an individual disciple of Jesus, responds to others the way God responds?

A step that is immediately accessible and has provided great rewards for our ministry in Atlanta is learning to respond with deep empathy. Notice how Yahweh responds to the Hebrew slaves in Egypt: "The LORD said, 'I have indeed seen the misery of my people in Egypt. I have heard them crying out because of their slave drivers, and I am concerned about their suffering. So I have come down to rescue them'" (Ex. 3:7–8a).

> Our world is desperate for Christians who know how to respond *to* the heart of the world rather than respond *with* the heart of the world.

Rather than pointing out all the failures of Israel, their ancestors, and Moses's own checkered past, God speaks with love and concern. His response is straightforward: Israelite Lives Matter! This doesn't mean they are perfect, or that Egyptian lives do not matter. But this is how God would respond to the cries that Black Lives Matter. Not all of the Israelites were of noble character. Moses himself killed a man without due process! But the Lord still heard the cries of his people. Many are quick to focus on the worst characters associated with a movement like Black Lives Matter and then categorically dismiss and demean the rest of the group and their legitimate concerns. Our world is desperate for Christians who know how to respond *to* the heart of the world rather than respond *with* the heart of the world. Of course, the Lord calls the people of Israel to account for their sins, but their sins do not cancel his compassion. Surely the church that follows a God like this will be part of the solution.

Luke, the doctor, writes an account of the gospel that gives us the Jesus version of Yahweh's heart. He recounts a story in 7:11–17 about a widow who is wailing over the loss of her only son. Jesus steps into the pain wrenching this woman's heart, and then he steps into the penalty of touching her dead son's body. Where uncleanness causes others to recoil, Jesus restores life, joy, and celebration. The response of the crowd says much about the inner longings of their heart. "God (Yahweh) has come to help his people." Surely the church that follows *this* Jesus will be part of the solution.

Twenty-First Century Help from a First Century Church

This might be an ancient name for our current crisis. Because of economic, ethnic diversity, status, and power, the Corinthian church immortalized by two epistles in the New Testament provides a unique comparison to our twenty-first-century Western culture. Our own path to healing may become clearer when we see that those early Christians in Corinth are in the spiritual emergency room when Paul begins to diagnose and treat their illness. As we study ourselves through this text he wrote to them, I want to offer two crucial clues:

1. First, they are not us, and we are not them, but our sickness is the same. As you work your way along this path of biblical discovery, take note of their context, but don't get lost in it. These passages were written to them and for them, *but they can transform us as well.*

2. Second, we must always ask, "What is behind the issue Paul is addressing?" It is not hard to follow Paul's outline. He is addressing problems and questions they wrote to him about. Chloe has informed him (1 Cor. 1:11), someone has reported to him about them (5:1), he has already written to them (5:9), and they have replied to him (7:1). As he addresses their symptoms, *he is seeking their healing from what is making them so sick*. As we study, look carefully for the illness the symptoms point to.

These clues are illustrated in the first text we'll look at together. (Note: I will not make an extensive study of every lengthy passage, but I want to illustrate in this first one the importance of digging into the message to discern the meaning and then to apply it to our own lives for healing.)

You may have studied 1 Corinthians 6:1–8 before reading it here. Maybe you were trying to find biblical guidance about the implications for legal action in regard to another believer. This is potentially a gut-wrenching dilemma for any Christian, but it is only a symptom of the greater illness. Notice the key words I have chosen to highlight in this text.

> If any of you has a dispute with another, *do you dare to take it before the ungodly* for judgment instead of before the Lord's people? Or do you not know that the Lord's people will judge the world? And if you are to judge the world, are you not competent to judge trivial cases?
>
> Do you not know that we will judge angels? How much more the things of this life! Therefore, if you have disputes about such matters, *do you ask for a ruling from those whose way of life is scorned in the church*? I say this to shame you. Is it possible that there is nobody among you wise enough to judge a dispute between believers?

> But instead, one brother takes another to court—*and this in front of unbelievers*!

What did you notice first? Did you solve the mystery of what it means that God's people will judge angels? Did you look around your church in an attempt to figure out who you might trust to apply a spiritual ruling to your legal dispute? You may have felt stung by Paul's suggestion that these cases are "trivial."

But what is Paul's theme? What drum is he beating? His great concern is the reputation of the gospel in the world, and the church is the key to the gospel's standing. It seems ludicrous to Paul that any earthly matter would be elevated among the people of God so as to compromise the potential of the gospel.

But an even deeper layer to their illness is the reasoning behind the choices they are making. Their public litigation reveals the private contamination of their relationships. Notice that Paul, like a good doctor, delivers the bad news in all its scope and severity.

"The very fact that you have lawsuits among you means you have been completely defeated already," Paul tells them. "Why not rather be wronged? Why not rather be cheated? Instead, you yourselves cheat and do wrong, and you do this to your brothers and sisters."

Of the many viruses infecting the body of Christ in Corinth, their blindness to their own condition is the most serious. They are deathly ill, but they believe themselves to be the picture of health. This exasperates the apostle Paul, to say the least. How do they not see this? They seem so blatantly obtuse, but in them I can see myself! When I categorically dismiss the value of another person and then believe I am justified in doing so, I am oozing spiritual infection. Consider all the doctrines I have to abandon in order to justify my withering criticisms of others.

1. I believe all humans are the product of divine creation.

2. I believe Jesus died on the cross to save people from their sins, and this includes saving me from my sins.
3. I believe in treating others as I would have them treat me.
4. I believe I am commanded by God to love him, my brothers and sisters, my neighbors and my enemies—no exceptions.

How can we claim to not be sick if these key markers of spiritual health are not present? For example, if I make a big deal about being a Bible-believing conservative Christian in the Lord's church and then bash other people with vitriolic criticism, how am I missing the flashing red light that my vitals are falling and I'm about to code?

This is the same problem identified by Jesus when he says to the Laodiceans, "You say, 'I am rich; I have acquired wealth and do not need a thing.' But you do not realize that you are wretched, pitiful, poor, blind, and naked" (Rev. 3:17). Like our spiritual ancestors in Corinth, we can't hope to be viewed as a solution if we do not first own our own problems.

The Corinthian Heart Defect

The apostle Paul documented this crisis in the Corinthian church. Let's read 1 Corinthians 13:1 in the New International Version, and then look at it again in Eugene Peterson's *The Message*.

> If I speak in the tongues of men or of angels, but do not have love, I am only a resounding gong or a clanging cymbal. (NIV)

> If I speak with human eloquence and angelic ecstasy but don't love, I'm nothing but the creaking of a rusty gate. (THE MESSAGE)

Resounding gong, clanging cymbal, creaking of a rusty gate? We might say fingernails on a chalkboard. Paul is describing an irritating church, one that grates on your nerves. But what is making this church so annoying? It isn't their stand on morals, or their monotheistic theology, or their personal weaknesses. All of this matters. Paul actually addresses all of them in this letter. But their problems in these areas are symptoms of something more sinister, more basic, and more encompassing.

These church members feel like nails on a chalkboard because they lack Christ-conditioned love. And this deficit matters most because this is what they are supposed to be all about. Production managers are supposed to produce. Presidents are expected to preside. Customer service reps are supposed to serve customers. The church, birthed in the love of God, is supposed to love. A church that doesn't have love is not just powerless. It is irritating!

A church without love is powerless and irritating!

The Tale of Two Churches

Emanuel African Methodist Episcopal Church in Charleston, South Carolina, is a love-conditioner. On July 17, 2015, a white male, Dylann Roof, murdered nine black worshipers in this church. Major Naomi Broughton of the Charleston Police Department helped coordinate the response in the shooting's aftermath. A year later she said, "I've never seen the multitude of victims as forgiving as this. . . . But there were a lot of angry people. I was angry. I don't know if I would have been as gracious as those family members were."

Westboro Baptist Church in Topeka, Kansas. Their history is hate, their legacy is pain, and their mission is malice. In the BBC documentary *The Most Hated Family in America*, filmmaker Louis Theroux questioned the church's longtime outspoken spokeswoman Shirley Phelps-Roper as to whether she had considered that Westboro's technique of protests was more likely to "put people *off* the word of Jesus Christ and the Bible." Phelps-Roper responded, "*You* think our job is to win souls to Christ? All we do, by getting in their face and putting these signs in front of them and these plain words, is make what's already in their heart come out of their mouth." Later in the documentary, Phelps-Roper agreed that the two hundred thousand dollars this church annually spends to fly to funerals to protest was money spent to "spread God's hate." Yes, that is a quote!

Does anyone reading this really think that the world needs more annoying churches or Christians? Is *too little hate* really our problem? Did God so hate the world that he sent his only Son?

The pastors, preachers, and parishioners I know want their churches to make Jesus famous. They want to fill their communities with his glory, redemption, and transformation. Emanuel AME Church challenged the norm of how churches, and people in general, respond to attacks, persecution, and even martyrdom. Westboro Baptist seems to be on the far end of that spectrum. But both churches can teach us something about love. One shows the message of God conditioned by hate, while the other shares the message of God conditioned by love. Air conditioning changes the atmosphere of a room, and we can tell the difference. People can tell when our churches are conditioned by love.

Healing with Bridge Building

When Ruby Bridges went to the William Frantz Elementary School on November 14, 1960, a bridge was being built behind her. Ruby was the only child on day one. Day two brought two more children, and one of them was the five-year-old daughter of a young pastor named Lloyd Foreman. He and his family decided they could not go along with the hate-filled masses, and he brought Pam back to school. They were not accompanied by marshals—they marched past the gauntlet without protection—receiving the full wrath of the crowd.

Famous author John Updike wrote in the *New Yorker* about the situation on December 10 of that year:

> Last week Rev. Lloyd Foreman and Mrs. Daisy Gabrielle were shown in the newspapers in the act of escorting their daughters to a New Orleans elementary school . . . holding the hands of small white-faced little girls named Pamela and Yolanda, while behind them segregationist banshees scream obscenely and the outraged hate of millions of Southern fellow-parents focuses on them. We have become familiar with the heroism of the Negro children who each autumn carry the tide of equal rights a little deeper into the South.

Because of their choice, both the Foreman and the Gabrielle families faced a lot more problems than just the daily walk past screaming women. Later in life, Pam Foreman reflected on the experiences she and her family had gone through:

> "Protesters holding Bibles often surrounded the parsonage, sometimes even throwing rocks at the family pet, which was black and white and thus 'an integrated dog,'" she said. "And they'd tell Daddy to go live in the French Quarter with all the crazy people and that they'd find a place for me." After one too many bomb threats at the house, the family began staying with other ministers, moving from house to house. "We couldn't check into a hotel, because no one would take us," Foreman said. Protesters even waited outside Lloyd Foreman's church on Sundays, and at one point people threw lightbulbs filled with creosote at the building.

Ruby, Pam, and Yolanda heard hateful words, spewing primarily from the mouths of young mothers and grandmothers. Ruby blessed our church with a visit in July 2016. I had the opportunity to interview her and to explore this display of irony: Scripture-toting, foul-mouthed women screaming obscenities and death threats at little first-grade girls. Ruby's response was profoundly Christlike: "I don't think they saw a little girl. I think they only saw what they thought was being taken from them."

Her statement, delivered in her exquisite manner, was doubly powerful: their hatred juxtaposed with her love, their blind rage laid bare by her keen insight, their *un*conditioned reproach on the faith in comparison with her Christ-conditioned respect. The difference could not have been more striking.

Begin the Healing Today

The church as envisioned by Jesus has enormous potential for good. But to touch the world at the level Jesus intends requires trust. Trust is a matter of character *and* competence. The world should hold Christians to a high standard, but not to one higher than we hold for ourselves. Grace is not a pass for bad behavior. The love Christ has for us compels us to manifest a quality of human generosity and kindness that surpasses what any law could legislate. When we claim to belong to Christ, others should expect to experience something special through us.

Some will complain, "Well, you can't expect me to be perfect. We all have our weaknesses, you know." I agree. I stand at the front of that line. But there is a different issue at stake. Notice how James addresses this. "If you harbor bitter envy and selfish ambition in your hearts," he instructs us, "do not boast about it or deny the truth. For where you have envy and selfish ambition, there you find disorder and every evil practice" (3:14, 16).

We have been cultivated by a religious tradition that elevated differentiating doctrinal statements over the deferential love of Christ. As a result, we banked on doctrinal clarity instead of dependable charity. We are called to compassion, not to condescending critique. The marginalization of the church is not rooted primarily in our lost boldness, or in lagging zeal, but in our lack of love.

Embedded in this diagnosis is a clue about God's plan for treatment. Somehow love is going to be the key. But love is hard, and many spiritual placebos are offered to believers as a quick fix for what ails the church. In the next section, we will take a serious look at the role played by our creeds—written and unwritten. I'm going to argue that we must restore to our creed the one missing component that Christ said makes all the difference.

Love-First Reflections

- Read 1 Corinthians 6:1–6. How does the example of the public lawsuits in the Corinthian church serve as a warning to us today concerning the perception in our world that the church has been unwilling to face its own racism?

- Have you ever witnessed an "irritating church"? How did their behavior affect the "reputation" of the gospel within their community?

- Which characteristic of Christ has had the greatest impact on you: His *doctrinal clarity* or His *dependable charity*?

- How does the indictment, "The marginalization of the church is not rooted primarily in our lost boldness or in lagging zeal, but in our lack of love" compel you? Or does it?

Part 2

THE DIVINE LOVE INTERVENTION

3

LOVE-LESS CREEDS

"No creed but Christ."

Creed comes from the Latin word *credo*, and means "I believe." If you have beliefs, you have a creed. A creed is your written or unwritten statement of what you believe. The original purpose of a *Christian* creed was to provide a doctrinal statement of correct belief, or orthodoxy. The creeds forged by the early church were written as guides for discerning truth from error, differentiating orthodoxy from heresy. Creeds summarize the basic ideas that make one Christian, but they also should offer the hope of a shared faith and unified fellowship.

Seeds, Weeds, and Creeds

To borrow C. S. Lewis's classic definition, most creeds express a sense of "mere Christianity"—core beliefs. Attempts to articulate a shared core of correct doctrine meant that our faith's forefathers hoped to plant pure seeds of faith while clearly marking the weeds of falsehood. Their endeavors met brutal opposition. Nothing less than eternal salvation was on the line, they were convinced, but they also hoped that all believers could unite in a common confession of these core components of Christianity. So for generations Christian leaders have attempted to forge a shared creed that calls for doctrinal purity and relational unity.

No doubt you have noticed, however, that unity among Christians isn't as easy as writing and reciting a creed. The diversity represented in our global faith makes unity a terrific challenge, to say the least. The faces, places, and spaces of our faith at times can seem so foreign that we wonder if a fellow believer is a Christian at all. When Christian leaders from southern Europe met the ancient Christians of North Africa, for example, they barely considered them human, let alone real Christians. One French missionary reported his assessment that the Coptic (Egyptian) Christians "are a strange people far removed from the kingdom of God. . . . Although they say they are Christians, they are such only in name and appearance. Indeed, many of them are so odd that outside of their physical form scarcely anything human can be detected in them." In a curious reversal of judgment, though, another European missionary noted that the Ethiopian Christians "are possessed with a strange notion that they are the only true Christians in the world; as for us, they shunned us as heretics."[1] The blade of disunity cuts both ways.

A macabre humor lurks in their mutual disdain. But, to advance our discussion, it must be noted that these groups who barely saw a hint of Christ in each other were reciting the same creed.

So how do creeds function, and what have they done?

Creed Control

Most Christians are familiar with a basic set of beliefs articulated in the Apostles' Creed. The first official mention of an apostles' creed is found in a letter from the church father Ambrose to Pope Siricius around 390 AD. Not every line was exactly as the earliest

Christians would have written it, but most suggest that the basic ideas contained in the creed were well known as early as the late second century. One of the more famous versions of the Apostles' Creed is found in the *Anglican Communion Book of Common Prayer* (1662), later updated in 2000 and used in common worship:

> *I believe* in God, the Father Almighty, creator of heaven and earth.
>
> *I believe* in Jesus Christ, his only Son, our Lord, who was conceived by the Holy Spirit, born of the Virgin Mary, suffered under Pontius Pilate, was crucified, died, and was buried; he descended to the dead. On the third day he rose again; he ascended into heaven, he is seated at the right hand of the Father, and he will come to judge the living and the dead.
>
> *I believe* in the Holy Spirit, the holy catholic* Church, the communion of saints, the forgiveness of sins, the resurrection of the body, and the life everlasting.
>
> Amen.
>
> (*catholic in this sense means *the church universal* and does not specifically mean the Roman Catholic Church)

Although there are other famous creeds with some differences in language that are extremely important to different groups of Christians, the Apostles' Creed is the benchmark for all believers worldwide. There is no substantive difference between the creed recited in Catholic Churches, Lutheran, Anglican, or most other major faith communions.

The Creed for Which I Plead

I recognize the sacredness of the creed, and equally the great cloud of witnesses who first gave themselves to the Lord and then to us in this priceless gift. I love and believe the creed. When I read or recite it, my soul is refreshed with incomparable peace, joy, and fellowship with the eternal faith. When I confess the creed, I relive my rebirth. My liturgy is rooted in and flourishes because of the creed in all its brute strength and gentle echoes of God's beating heart. This is my faith, our faith.

For my sisters and brothers who would like to whack me upside the head with some church history, I also walk in your world with passionate intrigue. Jenkins and Jacobsen are my steady diet. McGrath, Lossky, Barth, and Gonzalez cue the questions that the creed clarifies. I say with you, "I believe. . ." But along with you, I am cut to the heart as I read the blood-stained history of our creed-believing church. From Edessa to Armenia, from the Middle Passage to Rwanda, we are haunted by the Christ-betraying history of the creed-quoting church. Does the creed play *any* role in this?

Pen and Parchment

One of my professors in grad school gave an illustration that fits our dilemma. As he stood in front of the class with a large piece of white poster paper, he invited us to call out the foundational doctrines of the Christian faith. We talked and he wrote in the language of seminarians . . . "Christology, pneumatology, soteriology, eschatology," and several more "ologies"! The list was long. But then an astute student asked, "How does theology fit in?" Dr. Miller replied, "*It is the paper* on which all of these are written."

His illustration is powerful. The concise *creed points to the greater narrative of God*. Church historians rightly argue that God in his fullness shines through every line. But is something missing from the creed—something crucial—that speaks to our history of hate, racism, bigotry and disunity?

Church history, however, reveals more than the great narrative of our faith-filled forefathers. In every century from the first to the twenty-first, some who quote the creed practice audacious evil *and still believe they are right with God.* We have politicians and preachers who claim the creed in one breath and then pollute the conscience of our national community in the next. I believe the creed has been leveraged in this unholy history. I believe history lends weight to this conclusion.

First-Century Jewish Faith

The first-century Jewish world into which Jesus came recited the Shema, the core of their creed, daily. Along with this profession of love for God, the Levitical mandate of neighbor love was held as its covenantal complement. There is one God, always new, ever ancient, never changing. There is no dispensational shift between the Yahweh of Malachi and the Abba Father of the Gospels. When Jesus invited an expert in the Law to articulate the apex of the Hebrew Scripture, this *nomikos* (the Greek word for lawyer) recited the now-combined Shema and Levitical neighbor-love mandate into one confession. The answer is love of God and neighbor. Torah gushes with the love of Yahweh to a thousand generations!

But the passage (Mark 12:28–31) and Jesus's interaction with the creedal expert do not end there. This is actually the hinge of the story: a man who knows the creed wants to gut it of its social implications for mercy and justice. He wants to edit the creed at the level of application, but Jesus is not having it.

In fact, this is Jesus's central theme. At the heart of his most incisive evisceration of the Pharisee's necrotic faith, he reminds his disciples to keep the creed their religious leaders teach, but they must not follow their example of omitting what makes the creed powerful and life-changing. *The problem was not what was in the creed but what they were leaving out.* They were neglecting what was supposed to be assumed. The words on the scrolls of their Scriptures were not making it into how they lived their lives.

Many of Jesus's conversations, teachings, and parables target this incomplete reciting of the creed that truncated how they were reading Scripture.

- The rich young ruler assumes keeping the Ten Commandments is enough.
- The rich man assumes that love for poor Lazarus is optional.
- The older brother assumes obedience mitigates love for father and brother.
- The Pharisee assumes that his Law-keeping is the eternal differentiator between him and the humble tax collector.

These examples from Jesus's ministry illustrate that omitting the Love-First doctrine from the core creed we quote inevitably results in a drift from the mutually beneficial relationships God intended for his creation. The creed becomes sacramental but loses the relational. Rather than a recalibration toward the "for-otherness" image in which we were created, the creed begins to function as an incantation devoid of transformation.

Eternity in the Balance

The three famous Christian creeds (Apostles', Nicene, and Athanasius) were all written for spiritual offense and defense. They were meant to faithfully share the identity of God-in-Christ to the world, but also to defend against false narratives. The Apostle's Creed and the Nicene Creed were both called/named the "Symbol." *Symbol* in their day meant "*identifier*." This is how you identified with the faith. This is also how you could be identified as belonging to the true faith.

As controversies and heresies continued to arise, Athanasius drilled down on the essential doctrines of God and Christ, but he added stern warnings at the beginning, middle, and end of his creed:

Introductory Admonition: "Whosoever will be saved, before all things it is necessary that he hold the catholic (universal) faith. Which faith except every one do keep whole and undefiled; without doubt he shall perish everlastingly. And *the catholic* [*universal*] *faith is this . . .*"

Summary Admonition after articulating the Trinitarian Creed: *He therefore that will be saved, let him thus think* of the Trinity.

Second Introductory Admonition: "Furthermore, it is necessary to everlasting salvation; that he also believe faithfully the Incarnation of our Lord Jesus Christ. *For the right Faith is*, that we believe and confess; that our Lord Jesus Christ, the Son of God, is God and Man."

Final Summary Admonition: "*This is the catholic* [*universal*] *faith*; which except a man believe truly and firmly, he cannot be saved."

Note that without apology Athanasius clarified "*this is the faith*," and this is what you must believe and *keep whole and undefiled* in order to be eternally saved and avoid everlasting death.

With all respect for the majesty of the creed, I do not believe it can be overstated that the common believer held to *these* words for eternal life. While it is true that church fathers then, and pastors, liturgists, and historians now, can "read" love in every word of the creed, the common believer in all the intervening centuries *practiced what is written, not what is meant to be assumed.* They were reciting the words, not reading the parchment.

I believe this omission, with no conscious attempt to truncate the great commands, is where both the problem *and* the hope lie. When we choose not to include Jesus's first and greatest commandments in the creed, we unexpectedly contribute to the coarse and dangerous culture in which the church is clearly complicit. But when we restore his Love-First creed to its rightful place, we restore the hope that we can end hate before it is too late, beginning with the church.

My plea is not for changing the Apostles' Creed, nor for omitting it from our liturgy. This would be an incalculable loss. I am pleading for a serious and studied submission to what Jesus himself said must come first. He is not ambiguous in the least about the prioritized position of Love First in *his* creed, and we as bearers of his image must be equally unambiguous in our confession and profession of Love First.

As Jesus himself clarified, we must restore the omission to fulfill our commission.

> A new commandment I give to you, that you love one another, even as I have loved you, that you also love one another. *By this all men will know* that you are My disciples, if you have love for one another. (John 13:34–35 NASB, emphasis mine)

A Creed in Need

The large percentage of Christian believers for the first eighteen centuries of Christianity did not have access to formal education or to a personal copy of the Bible. The creeds, along with music and art, were of the utmost importance to conveying, and then confessing, the faith. Embracers of a creed were pinning their eternal hopes on whatever their creed held up as essential. This meant that evangelism was rooted in convincing people to receive the truth of the creed, but it also meant defending your creed and stamping out competing creeds. This often resulted in wars and rivers of blood shed in the name of Christ.

In the late eighteenth and nineteenth centuries, many Christians began to hold creeds and church confessions responsible for the division in the body of Christ. With blazing zeal they vigorously campaigned against the written creeds of Europe's established churches, calling for unity in Christ with the Scriptures as their only guide. The advent of mass literacy and the dissemination of Bibles throughout the world seemed to usher in the dawn of a new age where creeds would become irrelevant, no longer separating Christians from each other. Individual believers and local churches could examine the Word of God for themselves, restoring the faith and practice of the ancient church. This Restoration Movement held up the Scriptures as the only authority for doctrine and practice.

Under the slogan, "No creed but Christ," they preached compelling sermons that fueled the great revivals of Europe and America. It was long overdue to lay down these creeds and unify around nothing less than Christ himself and the Holy Writ. But this anti-creedal movement had one glaring flaw that was nearly impossible to diagnose from within: their *unwritten* creeds became as binding and divisive as all the written creeds put together.

I've visited churches in other countries where members and ministers alike walked on eggshells when Americans came to visit. Some of these indigenous preachers were strongly warned by their American guests about the version of the *English* Bible they should be using! Others were told that clapping their hands or shouting to the Lord during worship was not *decent* or *in order* for worship—in cultures where these are common and beautiful expressions of genuine joy and praise. There was no room for discussing different practices or interpretations of Scripture. Disagreement on these points meant losing support or even being marked as false teachers. How did these issues slip into our creed while love somehow slipped out?

One of my buddies told me about a relative who was an elder in a small church. One Sunday morning the youth in his church broke the church's "no-clapping creed" by applauding after a baptism. Later in the day when this elder was asked what he thought of the outbreak of praise celebrating the baptism, he replied, "We're gonna put a stop to that [expletive deleted]!" Yes . . . clapping is out, but cussing is in! *But he was living by his creed.*

No matter what we may think about versions of the Bible or clapping during worship, you and I run the risk of being *controlled* and *consoled* by the assumption that our creed is correct—in every way. But this leads to an undiagnosed arrogance, stating that anyone who doesn't share our creed is wrong at best, or is an intentional false teacher at worst.

Most of these humanly discerned creeds (what Jesus called "rules made by men") are believed to be rooted in nothing less than the inspired Word of God. They are held to be the result of intellectual honesty and the only true conclusion available to the honest seeker. Anyone who suggests an alternative conclusion or simply questions the accepted doctrine might be characterized as (a) intellectually dishonest, (b) concerned only with what is popular, relevant, or entertaining, (c) not a true seeker of truth, or (d) a liberal who doesn't believe the Bible is the inspired Word of God.

Many, especially those who have applied spiritual muscle to their Bible study, shovel condescension on those who disagree with their conclusions. They assume a posture of superiority, benevolently critiquing the good-hearted-yet-deceived people in other churches who are just not intellectually honest enough to accept the plain truth. And I understand this thinking. Surely if I connect the dots in my own Bible study, anyone who connects the dots differently, or doesn't make the connections that seem so obvious to me, must be wrong. Sound familiar?

Those who wrote our ancient creeds wanted to faithfully represent God in truth while exposing error. I do believe that many who espouse unwritten creeds are attempting the same praiseworthy outcome. Here I am not primarily concerned with your exact exegesis on specific issues, but I am bent on exposing the arrogance that takes root in the soil of love-less creeds.

Leaving Out Love Is a Big Deal

When I realized that not one of the ancient creeds mentioned the word "love," I wondered to myself, "Is this really a big deal?" I know that, for Jesus, love is the most important qualitative description of God. I also realize that the historic creeds were written to describe what Christians should *believe*, not how they should *behave*. But this was his first command and most rigorous demand. Love for God, neighbor, *and enemy* were so important that he creedalized them in his teachings. Christian author Scot McKnight's book *The Jesus Creed: Loving God, Loving Others* paved the way for us to think about creeds as standards for our hearts as well as our heads. As we explore this idea, consider what it could mean if believers were willing to restore the priority and practice of love exactly as Jesus taught it in his creed.

Christian author Scot McKnight's book *The Jesus Creed: Loving God, Loving Others* paved the way for us to think about creeds as standards for our hearts as well as our heads.

Love was not codified in the creed confessed by Christians throughout the last seventeen centuries. The creed captures the core essentials of truth necessary for salvation. Yet believers have killed other believers who were quoting the exact same confession. Religious infighting among creed-confessing Christians is a documented dark blot on the history of Christ's church. Millions of lives were lost and incalculable influence was squandered with the watching world. So yes, it is a big deal!

Did Christ Have a Creed?

In the Mark 12 passage mentioned earlier in this chapter, that expert in doctrine listens in on a conversation between Jesus and some other religious leaders, and he decides to join the fray. His question to Jesus isn't generic. This religious lawyer wants more than just the facts of what Jesus believes; he also wants to nail down what Jesus considers most important. Jesus's response in this passage offers three insights into his orthodoxy:

1. The specific question to Jesus is, "Of all the commandments, which one comes first?" or, "Which is the most important?" This isn't a question to determine if there is only one commandment, but rather, *which command takes the lead* in the formation of all doctrinal orthodoxy?
2. Jesus restates part of the question in his answer: "The command that comes first," or "The most important one is. . . ." Then he takes his inquisitor to the Shema, the core confession of faith quoted by Jews twice daily: "Hear, O Israel: The LORD our God, the LORD is one. Love the LORD your God with all your heart and with all your soul and with all your strength" (Deut. 6:4–5).

   Jesus then couples this with the command to "love your neighbor as yourself" (Lev. 19:18). It is important to note that, for Jesus, these two passages together form *one* command, and there is none greater (Mark 12:31).
3. Jesus speaks the truth of Scripture. The scribe wisely affirms the creed Jesus declares. Jesus's answer is clear: Love First *is* his creed. Rooted in Scripture, loving God and others is the litmus test of belief in the Christ-creed. If you do not love first, nothing after that counts.

Digging in to the Love-First Christ-Creed

In 1978 my parents took my cousin and me to Seattle to see the King Tut exhibit that was touring America. The boy-king was all the rage. People clamored to get a glimpse of the greatest find in modern Egyptian archeology. We joined the line for tickets at 3 A.M. Those who were too far back in lines that stretched for city blocks were told by counters to go home and try another day. Once we got inside, the display was otherworldly. Nothing in my experience prepared me for the grandeur. Twenty-two years later I made my first of three trips to Egypt. Now I was at Tut's tomb! The Seattle exhibit was like a curio cabinet compared to Cairo's staggering spectacle of ancient artifacts. Digging yielded enormous rewards.

On my second trip to Egypt, the discovery of the tomb of Ramses' sons, known as KV5, was the hottest story. Dr. Kent Weeks had rediscovered the tomb in 1995, touching off the biggest sensation in Egyptian archeology since Howard Carter's unveiling of Tut's treasures nearly seventy-five years earlier. Dr. Weeks had fallen under the trance of Egyptology as a young boy, and now, after more than three decades of devotion to this land of Pharaohs, his efforts were rewarded with the largest find in Egyptian archeological history.

Not far from the entrance to Carter's famed find, I peered into the "new" dig from behind the ropes. I was imagining myself as Indiana Jones, when Dr. Weeks emerged from the entrance. Stunned at seeing the world-renowned digger himself, I called out, "Dr. Weeks!" Squinting out from under his floppy hat, he noticed a small group quickly gathering, so he graciously gave us a brief update and threw in some trivia about the find.

In his quest to find the lost tomb, Dr. Weeks ran into an unexpected obstacle. When Howard Carter was digging for King Tut's tomb in the 1920s, he had unknowingly dumped dirt and sand from his dig over the entrance of the tomb of Ramses' sons. This meant that in order to find the missing tomb decades later, Weeks would have to dig through layers of dirt added by his forefather and hero in the profession. Certainly, Carter would not have made Week's job harder had he known what he was doing.

Much like Carter and Weeks, we all have heroes in the faith who may have inadvertently obscured the Love-First creed under layers of personal religious priorities and particular church practices. It can be difficult to proceed with a study that reveals our ancestors' understanding of some doctrines to be incorrect or incomplete. I am certain that our forefathers did nothing intentionally to hinder our efforts to grow in the grace and knowledge of our Lord Jesus Christ. But like those who came before us, each generation, including our own, must do its own deep digging.

Love-First Reflections

- Read Mark 12:28–34. Was Jesus ambiguous concerning what he thought to be the most important doctrine?

- How did the omission of Jesus's Love-First doctrine from the ancient creeds create ambiguity for Christians regarding our responsibility to love others, especially our enemies?

- Identify areas in your life that ambiguity toward Jesus's Love-First creed has negatively impacted your influence for Christ in the world? Take a moment to journal this self-reflection.

- "Digging deeper" carries implications, not just for this present generation but also for the generation that will follow. How does the "uncovering" of Christ's "love first" creed offer hope to the ills within the church and within our societies?

4

THE RIGHT KIND OF LOVE

Christ's story about the "Good Samaritan" speaks to the better angels within us, even to those who question some of the claims of Jesus. The Good Sam parable in Luke's Gospel exposes hollow religiosity, redefines what it means to love a neighbor, and then inspires a courageous kind of unselfishness.

Let's look closely at the Love-First creed in what I will call "The Story of Jesus and the Jurist" (Luke 10:25–37). Before Jesus introduces Good Sam, a jurist in Jewish law tests Jesus's orthodoxy by asking how he can be assured he will inherit eternal life. Jesus defers to the honorable challenger to make his case first. "What is written in the Law?" Jesus replies. "How do you read it?"

I am not exactly sure what it might feel like to this expert in Jewish canon law for the Rabbi to defer interpretation to him, but with enthusiasm he delivers both the Shema and the Levitical Law of neighbor love (Deut. 6:4–5 and Lev. 19:18) in one seamless response: Love for God and love for neighbor are inseparable, and they are preeminent in both priority and practice.

As is often the case, Bible study clues can get lost in translation. Like an archeologist, sometimes you must dig deeper to find these clues. It is in this text that I first came across the actual language of the Love-First creed. In the original language of this text, Jesus responds to this man's answer with the Greek word *orthos.* In essence, Jesus says to the jurist, "Your answer is *orthos* (Greek), or *orthodox.*" The expert has given the only correct answer. Then Jesus delivers the only acceptable response to divine orthodoxy: "Do this and you will live." If you want to have eternal life, you must get this right. If your love is not *orthodox*, then you lose out on eternal life. Love must come first—or you're a heretic!

When we cross-reference this story with the other Gospels, we notice that in many confrontations with the opposition, a jurist is called in to take on, or to *take out* Jesus. But in each of these encounters, another clue to understanding the Love-First creed emerges. In Matthew 22:35–40, for example, the jurist asks Jesus, "Which is the greatest commandment in the Law?" After quoting the Shema, as in Luke, Jesus adds a word to his answer that was not in the man's question: "This is the *first* and greatest commandment." What does Jesus intend by adding the word *first*? Could he mean first *in succession*? Maybe. Could he also mean first *as in priority*? Most certainly.

This guy must not have expected Jesus to nail the orthodoxy. But Jesus seizes the moment to further solidify love as the capstone of his creed: "All of the Law and the Prophets hang [*are suspended from, contained in, depend on*] these two commands." Jesus is teaching that love is the lifeblood of faith and practice. And remember, Jesus extends this love to enemies and persecutors (Matt. 5:43–48). Just as God's precipitation graciously falls on the just and unjust alike, so also will our love be noted for its nondiscriminatory generosity. When we do not love our enemies, we are standing in solidarity with the unbelieving, unconverted world. If we want to be identified with the children of heaven, religiosity must take a back seat to Love-First.

The New Command

When we turn to the Gospel of John, we hear a heartbeat. The pulse of God's heart can almost be felt in the words of Jesus's Beloved Disciple. John, writing decades after the ascension of Jesus, shares what Jesus told the Twelve that night before he was arrested and crucified. Two noticeable clues to the Love-First creed emerge in his recounting of the conversation: "A new command I give you: Love one another. As I have loved you, so you must love one another. By this everyone will know that you are my disciples, if you love one another" (John 13:34–35).

The command is new, *brand new*. But how? The answer is in the conditions required to fulfill it: our love for others must mirror Christ's love for us in quality and quantity. As John expands on the Love-First creed, he roots it in our divine ancestry: "As the Father has loved me, so have I loved you. My command is this: Love each other as I have loved you. Greater love has no one than this: to lay down one's life for one's friends. This is my command: Love each other" (15:9, 12–13, 17). Only hours later the apostles would be imprinted with Jesus's "greater love" as he died on the cross. They were his friends. He didn't just get killed. He died loving them. As the weight of being loved that well settled into the hearts of the disciples, their love for one another became an extension of the way Jesus loved them. The Love-First creed of Jesus became the Love-First life of his disciples.

> Our love for others must mirror Christ's love for us in quality and quantity.

As John leads his churches through the attacks and trials of those who have abandoned the truth, he always reimmerses them in orthodoxy. They must get doctrine right if they are to combat error. But notice how John does this:

> It has given me great joy to find some of your children walking in the truth, just as the Father commanded us. And now, dear lady, I am not writing you a new command but one we have had from the beginning. I ask that we love one another. And this is love: that we walk in obedience to his commands. As you have heard from the beginning, his command is that you walk in love. (2 John 1:4–6)

In a shout-out to his own Gospel, John now notes that this command to love each other is not a new command, but actually it is *the* old command. This is the command that started it all, from the beginning— the new command Jesus gave them the night before he gave himself. And just in case you can be a little slow like I am, John spells it out: "This is love." We are to walk in obedience to his commands, and the command is to walk in love.

Tough Love

The Roman Emperor Claudius expelled the Jews from Rome in the late 40s AD. For the church in Rome, this meant the Jewish Christians suddenly were exiled and the Gentile Christians were left behind to pick up the pieces. When the Jews did return to Rome under Nero several years later, they came home to a church with a distinct Gentile flavor. This wasn't wrong, but to the Jews it didn't *feel* right. Conflict kept them unsettled. Anyone who has been a part of church or family tension knows it can be tough to handle. We often want to run from the tension, or just make it go away. The discomfort of the disruption spills over into other parts of our lives. With every passing day it may seem that the relational chasm gets wider. But in the Roman letter Paul offers them a bridge of love, and in doing so he gives us further clues to the Love-First creed.

He tells them plainly that the ultimate form of obedience is found in loving each other. As you become excellent in following the Love-First creed of Christ, you will surpass every expectation of obedience to the commands of God. "Whatever other commands there may be," Paul writes, "[they] are summed up in this one command: 'Love your neighbor as yourself.' Love does no harm to a neighbor. Therefore love is the fulfillment of the law" (13:9b–10).

In this letter that tediously helps the Roman church understand the role and limitation of the Law of God, this paragraph is the last time the Law is mentioned. Paul has been building up to this trifecta of emphasis:

1. He who loves others fulfills the Law.
2. Every command is summarized in, "Love your neighbor as yourself."
3. Love is the fulfillment of the Law.

Paul paints a picture of love here, using the divine palette. God's love extends to enemies, to the difficult, and to the oppressive. Paul is effectively disassociating the word *love* from the superficial lip service that characterizes so many who claim the name of Christ. Love will take work and sacrifice. They are going to have to *toughen up* in order to love the way Christ loves. A weak commitment to love will result in a divided church and will create fractures in every other relationship that matters.

Another Love-Starved Church

The Galatian church is consumed in a contagious conflict. In their love-less fellowship, the only thing they do well is to pass on the virus of divisiveness. No stronger language shows up anywhere in the New Testament than the words Paul uses to describe the relational disaster that threatens their existence. They are told that their way of living is nothing less than anti-gospel, anti-Jesus, anti-Spirit, anti-life, and anti-love. It is a horrible situation, and Paul is torn up about it. But he loves them too much to abandon their sinking ship.

Paul doesn't spare the quill or ink in articulating the Galatians' doctrinal disarray. He is determined to help them see the Love-First creed, even in their catastrophic context, to guide them to the answers they so desperately need. "You have been called to live in freedom," he reminds them. "But don't use your freedom to satisfy your sinful nature. Instead, use your freedom to serve one another in love. The whole law can be summed up in this one command: 'Love your neighbor as yourself.'" Then the apostle warns them, "But if you are always biting and devouring one another, watch out! Beware of destroying one another." (5:13–15 NLT). Their freedom in Christ—freedom from a religion of checklists and minutia—was not meant to unhook them from the Love-First creed that bought them their salvation in the first place.

So how are they to sober up and start their spiritual recovery? They should start by channeling their self-satisfying energy into other-serving love. Rather than using their religious rituals as a way to abuse others and to elevate self, they should evaluate every single thought, motive, word, and deed by one single condition: "Am I loving my neighbor as I, myself, most need to be loved?" This is the practical application of the Love-First creed.

Brother Love

Every Tuesday morning my brother and I talk on the phone. Both of us are early risers, but he lives in Oregon, so I wait for his call at 8 A.M. Atlanta time. He's a grizzled construction worker who posted a sign at the entrance to his driveway: "The dog bites, the owner shoots. Pray you meet the dog first." But everyone knows Larry is a big softy when it comes to family. Over the years, his Tuesday morning call has come to mean everything to me. We laugh, catch up, moan about work, compare notes about how our mom is doing on her farm, and help each other with the things that matter most. I'm proud of my big brother, but I also love him, and he loves me. When we lost our dad, my brother, sister, and I were reminded that someday you will tell someone "I love you" for the last time. I've noticed that all of us are more intentional about closing our calls with, "I love you," and mom even says it three times!

I imagine Jesus's brother James could tell some stories of what it was like to grow up with Jesus as his big brother. I've wondered what it was like to go swimming or fishing with Jesus. If you went on a picnic, did you ever have to pack food? But when you read James's letter, you see that he "got" Jesus. No other letter in the entire New Testament bears such family resemblance. James is passionate about the law of God and how it is fulfilled in the Love-First creed of his older brother.

The descriptions of discrimination in their worship services sound sadly familiar (2:1–13). His instructions indict every layer of favoritism that destroys the life-giving love that should characterize the church of Jesus. When you first read his response to their social superficiality, you realize that this is serious business. He pulls no punches in clarifying that their dehumanization of others by favoritism is as damaging as adultery and as deadly as murder. James's words are incisive, economical, and abrasive. He begins by noting that discriminatory relationships separate us from genuine faith. They are incompatible with Christ Jesus, and there is no exception. James, like my brother, isn't known for being all touchy-feely!

James breaks down the Love-First creed into a seating chart. If we offer preferred seating to those who seem impressive to us and highlight the poor with bad seats, we and our judgments are evil. Yes, *evil.* When we do good for those we want to impress and shun those who seem of no consequence, we are guided by evil. And in this seemingly innocuous social encounter, there is a divine reversal: the person we shunned may have been God in disguise. Those we try to impress oppress us and slander Christ. James might say, "Congratulations, you elevated the Destroyer while destroying the Life-giver." C. S. Lewis observes in *The Weight of Glory*:

> Remember that the dullest and most uninteresting person you talk to may one day be a creature which, if you saw it now, you would be strongly tempted to worship . . . *There are no ordinary people.* You have never talked to a mere mortal. Nations, cultures, arts, civilizations—these are mortal, and their life is to ours as the life of a gnat. But it is immortals whom we joke with, work with, marry, snub, exploit—immortal horrors or everlasting splendors.[1]

Favoritism is rooted in the arrogance of self-importance. We imagine that those *we* favor will always be the best, and those *we* shun do not deserve better. This assumes that all of society and God himself should submit to the values we confer to others. Many accurately indicted Adolf Hitler's despicable racism when he refused to shake Jesse Owens's hand at the 1936 Berlin Olympics. But others have suggested that perhaps Owens didn't care to shake Hitler's hand because the athlete rejected the dictator's supremacist polemic. Against the sin of favoritism, James holds up Leviticus 19:18 and his brother's Love-First creed as doctrinal royalty. The churches James addresses want to call their favoritism *love*. James calls it *sin* (2:8–9).

Of course, there is always the temptation to suggest to God that one tiny little sin surely can't be as bad as the big ones, like adultery or murder. James's argument is straightforward: the royal law is summed up in the command of love, and the entire weight of guilt comes down on a single infraction. When we fail to uphold the Love-First creed, we will bear the consequences of the entire law. The commands come from God. Only he can determine their weight. Since he set the conditions of love, our only say in the matter is to accept them or reject them (2:10–11). But if we reject the conditions he has set for love, we are rejecting him.

Every time I read James 2, I am struck by its bare, stripped down, no-nonsense call to complete obedience. Discrimination locks us up in the same cell with the murderers and adulterers. The Judge will judge our partiality impartially. He will not hand down heavier sentences to murderers than to those who show favoritism. But where does this leave us? Are not the majority of us guilty of some form of discrimination or favoritism? Are we all hell-bound?

This wasn't really James's point at all. He had to smack us in the face with the truth about our arrogance and favoritism. Most everyone I meet claims they're the exception—they are not a racist/they had a minority friend in high school/no one respects women more than them/blah, blah, blah—but James is calling all of us onto the carpet. Even socially acceptable ways of being unfriendly toward those we do not favor make us guilty of favoritism.

Echoing Paul's appeal to the Galatians, James notes that there is another way—a law of freedom—a law rooted in equity, humility, and mercy. Consider this lively paraphrase of James 2:12–13:

> Talk and act like a person expecting to be judged by the Rule that sets us free. For if you refuse to act kindly, you can hardly expect to be treated kindly. Kind mercy wins over harsh judgment every time. (*The Message*)

He Loves Me . . . He Loves Me Not

Peter's journey with Jesus was filled with do-overs. His strength tripped him up. He was sure of himself, but at times unsure of God. I don't believe Jesus intended for him to sink in the waves, or to shrink in denial, but Peter did, and Jesus was there to pull him up. So when an older Peter is shepherding younger sheep, he knows to root them in nothing less, and nothing else, than God himself and his imperishable Word. Obedience to God's truth births a pure life, but the evidence for this transformation is in our sincere and deep love for each other.

Imagine yourself sitting on the rocks by the sea with a small band of believers while Peter shares his heart with us. He begins "Rid yourselves of all malice and all deceit, hypocrisy, envy, and slander of every kind"(1 Pet. 2:1). Our new birth is not intended just to right the wrong in our relationship with God. Our hearts are made new by the love of God so that others can benefit from the deep, heartfelt affection we have for them. This is made possible by the eternal Word of God overcoming the temporary false notions of this world. Any evangelistic message must be evaluated for its truthfulness by whether it calls us to love God and each other. Any "gospel" preaching that does not call for a bright red line of conversion in how we love our fellow humans is a false gospel, unfaithful to the eternal Word.

A Faith That Doesn't Spread Hate

Some movies surprise those who sit through all the credits with some bonus footage. Of the twenty-seven books of the New Testament, Jude often gets treated as bonus footage. He's close to the end of the New Testament, and very rarely studied. Like his brother James, he is both a brother and a servant of Jesus. "Jude, a servant of Jesus Christ and a brother of James," he begins his short piece. Then he addresses it: "To those who have been called, who are loved by God the Father and kept by Jesus Christ: Mercy, peace, and love be yours in abundance" (1:1–2).

Jude intends to write to them primarily about their shared salvation, but something is off track. Bad actors among them are doing great damage. Though they claim Christ, the lives of the bad guys are unconditioned by his love. These people have slipped in among them with brash and bombastic claims about their unconstrained lives. They claim the faith but remain unchanged by its conditions. Death follows closely on the heels of their influence. These people are like hidden traps and empty promises, Jude says.

He hauntingly exposes their hate at the feast of love. Like Judas in the upper room breaking faith while breaking bread, these deceitful saints in wolves' clothing are sucking the life out of the church.

Jude minces no words. While the situation for the beloved is dire in the present, these fault-finding, self-serving polluters of purity will face their certain judgment when the Archangel Michael and the Lord's advancing army crush them. This may sound harsh, but Jesus gave his life to create a new, unified humanity, and he will not remain passive when people following their own selfish wants seek to divide believers from each other.

But what are the believers to do in the midst of such conflict? They remember that Jesus predicted this, and he will prevail. The beloved build each other up and rely on the power of the Holy Spirit. God's love will be their refuge now and forever as he ushers them into eternal life. Rather than following flatterers down the path of destruction, the people of God battle for the hurting, the doubters, and the strugglers. Our love should press us so deep into the battle for the souls of the people around us that our clothes smell like smoke.

We have devoted this chapter to an in-depth study of the Love-First creed in the New Testament. There are eight recognized writers of the New Testament books who, inspired by the Spirit of God, shared the life and teachings of Jesus with all who put their faith in him. This was the requirement of the Great Commission. Jesus's disciples were to go into all the world and make disciples of everyone, baptizing them in the name of the Father, Son, and Holy Spirit, *teaching them to obey everything Jesus commanded them*. The first and greatest command given by Jesus is repeated by every writer of the New Testament without exception. The Love-First creed is the first and greatest command that every disciple must learn to obey.

Love-First Reflections

- Take the time to read the following passages of scripture: Matthew 25:40–45; Hebrews 13:2; and James 2:1–9. Have you ever reflected on an experience and wondered if you had encountered an angel? Or have you ever looked into another's eyes and wondered if you were looking into the eyes of Christ? If you believe the teachings in these passages, how does this impact the way you will prepare yourself to interact with others?

- Can you recall a time when you were treated of lesser value either because of race, economics, education, or gender within the family of faith? What is God teaching you about Love-First through your own painful experiences?

- If any gospel that does not call us to love our fellow human beings is actually a false gospel, what should we do? How does this perspective affect share the gospel and receive its message?

- Reread the final paragraph of this chapter and fill in the blanks below.

  "The first and ______________ command given by Jesus is repeated by ______________________________ of the New Testament without ___________________________."

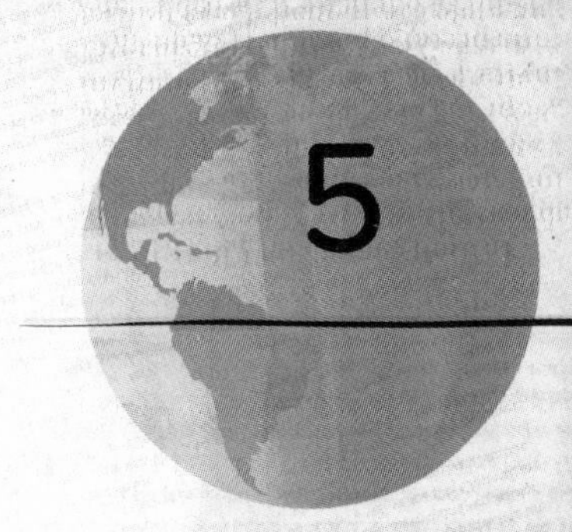

GOD-SHAPED LOVE

I know I'm not supposed to cuss, but it has been my lifelong nemesis. My second-grade teacher Mrs. Osterman was the first of many to try to wash this filth out of my mouth. After college, I went for years with a pretty good track record. I slipped occasionally, but overall my potty mouth was behind me. Then in 2007 it all came back. I was leaving a voicemail for Tom, a friend of mine from church, when I was rear-ended on a Friday evening in Atlanta rush-hour traffic. The anger that had been simmering in me for months erupted. I blurted out at this navigationally challenged idiot, "You [expletive deleted]!" In that split second of volcanic rage, I had forgotten what I was doing . . . and then I stared at my phone. Ahhhhhhhhhh!! It was still recording. I threw my phone. It was still recording. I picked it back up and punched #3, hoping it would erase my rant. It was still recording.

I was sick! Did I mention that I was on my way to a men's retreat weekend with the guys from church? Ugh!! I kept trying to call Tom throughout the evening, hoping to explain myself. I kept getting his voicemail. After a night of tossing and turning, I got a call from his wife Edie the next morning.

> Edie: "Hey, Don. I saw you called last night. Sorry we missed you. We were out of town till late. What's up?"
>
> Me: "Ummm . . . have you listened to your voicemails yet?"
>
> Edie: "No, why?"
>
> Me: "Well . . . uh . . . is there any chance that when you come to my message you could just erase it without listening?"
>
> Edie: (Giggling) "Well, not now!"
>
> Me: "Oh, good grief! Well, let me explain . . ."

They were such good sports about it all, and when I confessed the whole episode to our church the following Sunday morning, everyone laughed, including Tom and Edie. But on the inside I wasn't laughing. They didn't know what I knew—this was not an episode. My heart was dark and my foul mouth was simply the overflow.

Around the same time as my voicemail debacle, I was in a men's Bible study group every Monday morning at 6. An assignment near the end of our study included opening up about some specific struggles I was facing. So I decided to call my dad. I brought up the whole episode and revealed to him the full darkness in my soul. I was so discouraged. How could this all be coming back after I had been following Jesus for over twenty-six years at that time? Dad was a good listener and a patient processor. He reassured me that I was still loved by God and there was no reason to panic. He even shared some of his own struggles. But he also asked for some time to think about it.

About five weeks later, I received a handwritten letter from dad. He was a legendary letter-writer, but this letter was nearly eight pages of spiritual guidance. I want to give you the heart of his message to me, straight from his own hand: "Don, the problem

I see in you is that you are not living affectionately with God. You are living functionally with him, doing the things you believe are important to him. But the key to our life with God is our affection." My dad loved me beyond measure, and he wasn't trying to add salt to my wound. He knew that I needed a correct diagnosis in order to get well. He saw past my cussing mouth to a diseased heart. My profanity was symptomatic of a heart out of rhythm. I had placed too much weight on doing and saying religious things, but my affection for God had cooled to lukewarm. It happens when love gets less attention than Jesus said it deserves. I was singing about love, preaching about love, and calling others to receive God's love, but I was not fueling the fires of my affection for him.

Something more serious than a cussing preacher was at stake. I was not prioritizing the very thing that Jesus said would bring me life. It was Jesus who compared our affectionate life with him to a vine with branches. He said that apart from him we can do nothing, and for me this included no victory over a foul mouth. I was acting as if my affectionless relationship with Jesus still qualified as love. With my father's help, I learned that when love is not above all, it's not *divine* love at all.

We must define divine love so that we can know what it means to *love like God*. John, the apostle of divine affection, gives us this working definition: "This is how God showed his love among us: He sent his one and only Son into the world that we might live through him. This is love: not that we loved God, but that he loved us and sent his Son as an atoning sacrifice for our sins" (1 John 4:9–10). This is the shape of divine love. In its simplest form, Christianity is a movement to put flesh on Jesus. He is the first incarnation of God, but we are the second. We are his body in the world, and he lives in us and through us by the Spirit. His heart beats in our chest, his eyes see through ours, his voice is heard when we speak, and his welcome is felt through our embrace. We are the body of Christ . . . literally. When people see us, they are expecting to experience God through us. This is what it means to be God-shaped. This applies to every aspect of his life and ours . . . especially to love.

The person who claims to know God but does not love is dangerous. For them, undermining others by insinuation, suspicion, and slander is all covered by the rationalization that they are "speaking the truth in love." They are like spiritual terrorists who destroy relationships and reputations but disguise their actions under the false notion that God has called them to speak what they call truth, no matter how much pain it causes to others. But this is the spirit of falsehood. The apostle John reminds us that the person who says they love God but does not love their brothers and sisters is a liar and *the truth is not in them* (1 John 4:19–20). There is no precedent in the New Testament for demeaning others with slander in the name of "truth" and calling it an act of love. This is sin. If you label it love, you are a liar. This is the point James is making when he cautions,

God wrapped his love for us in Jesus so that we might see what divine love looks like in human form.

> Don't speak evil against each other, dear brothers and sisters. If you criticize and judge each other, then you are criticizing and judging God's law. But your job is to obey the law, not to judge whether it applies to you. God alone, who gave the law, is the Judge. He alone has the power to save or to destroy. So what right do you have to judge your neighbor? (4:11–12 NLT)

God wrapped his love for us in Jesus so that we might see what divine love looks like in human form. Christ lives in us and through us, reshaping us into his image. We are called to love others into this life-giving love of God. Ridicule and insult turn people from the love of God, because it misrepresents him as if he is misshapen. As noted earlier, this is the crisis we face.

Many years ago a student in our church was wrestling with his faith. Outwardly he was "keeping it together," but inwardly he was what Scripture refers to as a bruised reed with flickering faith. He seemed to be holding on, but then suddenly he was gone. Gone from youth activities. Gone from church. Gone from the faith.

His absence was immediately noticed. His grandparents wanted a meeting with our youth ministry. His parents considered changing churches. Something had to be wrong with the church. And something was wrong, but the problem was "church" a little closer to home.

I invited him to meet me at Starbucks. As he stared into his pumpkin spice latte, he reflected out loud about a conversation at a recent family gathering. He shared, "I'm so sick of all the love-talk at church and the hate-talk at home. Whatever happened to the Golden Rule I was taught in Bible class all my life? I hear them quote, 'Love the sinner and hate the sin,' but they give a pass to the people they like and the rest get blamed for the problems of the world. It makes me sick." His story is heartbreaking but not earthshaking. Why? Because it is happening in Christian families all across the country. He was another casualty—not unlike Hillary Ferguson—broken by the gap between creed and love. The gap in our creed turns doctrine into a weapon, and the wounded include our own sons and daughters.

The apostle John uses very strong language to clarify the difference between a hate-distorted life and God-shaped love. He writes, "Anyone who hates a brother or sister is a murderer" (1 John 3:15). His reference is the original murder in the human family (Gen. 4:2–13). Love-First could have saved both Cain and Abel. Had love sprung forth in Cain's heart, Abel's blood would not have seeped into the ground. Cain's hate is a seed still looking for fertile soil. It has found plenty of dirt today in which to grow its deadly fruit.

The apostle John contrasts Cain and Christ, rooting the difference in the Love-First creed. Cain's creed takes life, and Christ's creed gives life. The creed we live matters, especially when it comes to ending hate before it's too late.

The young man I just mentioned is now living a vibrant faith. I wanted you to know that, and also how his faith was restored. Because of the humility and faithfulness of his parents and grandparents, some honest conversations took place. Awareness was raised and change became purposeful. Our college ministry extended an authentic, Love-First welcome to him, but to others as well. He is a catalyst among his friends, many of whom are also giving God a second look. I believe it is Satan's intent that love always remains a secondary doctrine, meaningful in theory but lacking in concrete expression. This is not the way of Christ. His Love-First life was on full display in every private dinner and public healing. His life was love, and this is what the world still longs to experience through his body, the church.

Love-First Reflections

- How is it possible to "do right" and "say right" without "being" right? Why do you think Jesus makes such a big deal about getting love right?

- How would you describe where you are right now between *affection* and *function* in your relationship with God? Has there been a time when you felt closer to God? What are some steps you could take to rekindle your affection?

- How is claiming to know God but not living affectionately with God dangerous to you and others?

- "Anyone who hates a brother or sister is a murderer," is quoted as referencing Cain and Abel. Genesis 4:7 says sin "desires to have you, but you must rule over it." Read Romans 12:21. What are practical ways we can rule over and conquer hate?

6

THE LOVE-FIRST REFORMATION

The five-hundred-year challenge. On October 31, 1517, Martin Luther mailed a letter to his archbishop, and, as tradition holds, he also may have nailed the contents of that letter to the door of the All Saints' Church in Wittenberg, Germany. This is considered by most scholars and historians to be the birth of the Protestant Reformation. Luther and his fellow reformers had preached and pleaded for years, earnestly seeking a reform of some practices that alienated people from the very faith and fellowship they needed most. When what they believed became the breaking point, they took action. Church history is marked by other key turning points at which the future was irreversibly impacted. We are at such a juncture.

If you research this kind of thing, Internet searches will lead you down a thousand *call-to-reformation* rabbit holes. I am specifically referring to the reformation of our creed: Will we love first? The church has spent centuries elevating nearly everything above this doctrine, giving it lip service while sharing in the world's intoxication of hate. Yet it was our Founder, Jesus, who said this comes first, and everything—*everything*—hangs from this first doctrine. The church of Christ must decide if we will be reformed by his heart, life, and priority of love.

Conditions of Reformation

We must end hate before it's too late, but we must also avoid counterfeit love. We must clarify the authentic love of God. We must reshape our creed so that it can reshape us. As I noted above, there have been significant moments in the history of our faith when the statements, wording, and understanding of our creed have been challenged and changed. But this was, and is, never done lightly or in isolation, nor should it be. The case I am making in this book is based not on what is *in* the creed, but on what was left *out*. I am advocating that we establish love as our first priority which our Lord and Savior taught by his words and deeds. So let's do some Bible study together.

Eternal God, Eternal Love

God is eternal, and God *is* love. As a result, love must, by his nature, precede all things. His love is as eternal as he is. But when I ask people, "So what did God *do* first?" they will often quote something from Genesis about creation. Although I can't think of a better beginning point than Genesis, I do wonder if we have been reading these verses carelessly, not considering their full implications.

The biblical witness is clear that the Father, Son, and Spirit are one and eternally in communion with each other. There is no separation of being, nature, or character. Whatever the Father is, the Son and Spirit also are. As the one true and eternal God, all things that are have come from him. So to ask, "What did God do first?" might seem like a whimsical question. The material universe was created "in the beginning," so this would be first, right? Please consider the following five passages from the Bible (and note especially where I added italics):

> All who dwell on the earth will worship him, whose names have not been written in the Book of Life of the Lamb slain *from the foundation of the world.* (Rev. 13:8 NKJV)

> You were ransomed . . . not with perishable things like silver or gold but with the precious blood of Christ, like that of a lamb without defect or blemish. He was destined *before the foundation of the world*, but was revealed at the end of the ages for your sake. (1 Pet. 1:18–20 NRSV)

> He chose us in Him *before the foundation of the world*, that we should be holy and without blame before Him in love. (Eph. 1:4 NKJV)

> In the hope of eternal life, which God, who does not lie, *promised before the beginning of time*. (Tit. 1:2)

> Father, I want those you have given me to be with me where I am, and to see my glory, the glory you have given me *because you loved me before the creation of the world*. (John 17:24)

If God so loved the world that he gave his one and only Son, and this was all set in motion before the foundation of the world, then what did God do first? *God loved first.* The implications are profound. This means that before God created, called, commanded, convicted, and cast out (Gen. 1–3), he loved. He loved first. This is the bedrock truth of redemption, the central theme of all Scripture.

His love for us and our love for him are inextricably woven into his expectations of our love for each other. You can't get God right if you get his people wrong. "Whoever claims to love God yet hates a brother or sister is a liar. For whoever does not love their brother and sister, whom they have seen, cannot love God, whom they have not seen" (1 John 4:20). God does not recognize any creed where love is not the first and greatest command. "The only thing that matters is faith expressing itself in love" (Gal. 5:6). If we claim to love him, we are agreeing to his *conditions* that identify authentic love from the counterfeit.

Christians and their churches must draw a hard line in the sand concerning this doctrine and our obedience to it. Christianity isn't an open-share brand that can be slapped onto any set of proclamations, priorities, and practices. We are distinct in this world because his Love-First orthodoxy is the measurement for all we say and do. Churches and believers are faced right now with a very difficult choice. Will we order our lives according to our politics, religious affiliations, or social preferences, *or* will we submit to Jesus's creed? He has set the conditions for how his creed is to be understood and prioritized. If love is not first, both in *order* and *value*, then we have it wrong. Love-First is the creed of Christ. If Christ is our creed, then Love-First is our calling. We will devote every micron of our being to his love-first standard, by which we will measure all our orthodoxy.

If love is not first, both in *order* and *value*, then we have it wrong.

I mentioned earlier that something is missing in our creeds, and I asked you to imagine with me the impact of the omission of love. But now I want you to consider something quite different, something exciting, something that can launch a reformation of our personal lives, a revival in our churches, and a revolution in our world. We have been moving steadily to this point in the book, so now I need you to slow down and consider the Love-First creed. Each line is crafted directly from Scripture. I don't have ninety-five theses to nail to the door, but I'm offering eight that come straight from the heart of God.

The Love-First Creed

I believe that God is love.

I believe that God so loved the world that he gave his only Son so that the world may be saved through him.

I believe that God loved me when I was a powerless, ungodly sinner and enemy.

I believe that the first and greatest command is to love God with all that I am.

I believe that with the first and greatest command, I am to love my neighbor as myself.

I believe that I must love my enemies, the ungrateful, and the wicked.

I believe that if I claim to love God but do not love others, I am a liar.

I believe that when I see my brothers and sisters in need, I must help them with my material possessions, or the love of God is not in me.

Take a moment and read through these statements of faith:

Matthew 5:43–47
Matthew 22:37–38
Matthew 22:39–40
John 3:16
Romans 5:6–11
1 John 2:4
1 John 3:16–18
1 John 4:8–11, 19–21

Consider the life-changing, global-renovating impact of these beliefs. Faithfully confessing the Love-First creed restores Christ's words and his priorities to their rightful place, just as he proclaimed and lived them. His creed puts love first in both order and value, setting every other doctrine in its proper place.

So now dream with me. What if every Christian on the planet confessed *this* creed in worship and for discipleship? What if each syllable of this creed was considered essential to life everlasting? Isn't this the call we hear in 1 John 2:4 and 4:19?

You would have to deny the creed to discriminate against your neighbor. You would have to cast off the creed to curse your brother or sister. You would have to reject the creed to revile your enemy. You would have to abandon the core of your faith to crush another person with your withering criticism.

And the Love-First creed is not only from God, but it is the same standard to which he holds himself. "We love because he first loved us. And he has given us this command: Anyone who loves God must also love their brother and sister" (1 John 4:19, 21).

The Creed that Saves Lives—Theirs and Yours

Consider a practical application of the Love-First creed. What if every church and Christian in every nation applied the Love-First creed to the international refugee crisis? Refugees represent an astounding paradox for humanity. In some compelling way, we connect with refugees because we are refugees. The holy family became refugees in Jesus's infancy because of the genocidal whims of a despot. When we see pictures, watch videos, and hear their testimonials, our hearts are wrenched with grief.

What if every church and Christian in every nation applied the Love-First creed to the international refugee crisis?

Thomas Nybo is an internationally recognized and respected photojournalist who works for UNICEF. His work has been featured on CNN, Fox News, *USAToday*, the front page of the *New York Times* online, and a host of other news outlets. He and his beautiful family are members of our church, but for Thomas, the world is his family. On any given day or night you will find Thomas and his cameras in the heart of humanity's hurts. He is on a mission to love, liberate, and elevate everyone he meets.

During the continuing Syrian refugee crisis he traveled throughout the Middle East and Europe, often facing significant danger, documenting the refugees' war-torn homelands, their perilous trek, and their hope for safety and survival. The world was torn apart by this crisis. Such a monumental exodus and resettlement continues to present one of the most complex challenges of our generation. As the crisis mushroomed, streets, airports, and political centers were filled with protesters. Fears raged. Some were afraid for their personal safety and some for the safety of the refugees. Politicians gained and lost careers based on their refugee response. Even people of goodwill were torn about the solution. But one thing was clear: the *conditions* for these humans were unacceptable. Thomas's work helped put humanity back in the crisis. (This is not a new response to the suffering of refugees. Eric Morris, Special Envoy of the United Nations Commissioner for Refugees wrote, "*The conditions are simply unacceptable*," reflecting on the conditions suffered by refugees of the Third Balkan Wars [1991–2001].)

On September 2, 2015, a close-up picture of three-year-old Alan Kurdi nearly broke the Internet. His little lifeless body had washed up on a Turkish beach, and it was simply too much. Alan, his five-year-old brother, and nearly a dozen others had joined the more than four million refugees escaping the war. Over four hundred seventy thousand have died. The world is overwhelmed with compassion-fatigue, yet a little boy too young to be running from death was now face-down, cold on a beach. Alan Kurdi could not be ignored. The conditions were unacceptable.

Alan's aunt, Tima Kurdi, blamed the Canadian government for the death of her three-year-old nephew. She had submitted paperwork to sponsor his family, but her application was denied. She was not the only one who believed the world could do more. This could not be the best we have to offer.

But while stories of refugee heartache filled our news, the wheels of Canadian compassion began to turn. In March 2016, the eyes of the world were on Canada as that nation launched an ambitious Syrian refugee resettlement initiative identified with the hashtag, #WelcomeRefugees. As of June 2016, nearly thirty thousand refugees were being resettled all across Canada, most of them in private homes with welcoming families. I couldn't help but think of Psalm 68:6, "God places the lonely in families" (NLT).

With the Canadian government fully engaged, community and faith groups were empowering families to receive the refugees. The response was so overwhelming that Canada's Minister of Immigration, John McCallum, had to extend the application deadline. After the initial goal was met of bringing twenty-five thousand refugees to Canada, they opened their doors to another ten thousand. Responding to complaints from Canadian groups who wanted to sponsor *more refugees*, McCallum assured them, "We are doing everything we can to accommodate the very welcomed desire on the part of Canadians to sponsor refugees."

World leaders gathered in Geneva, Switzerland, on March 30, 2016, to discuss the refugee crisis. All eyes were on Canada. McCallum was to be a key presenter at the United Nations conference attended by eighty countries, ten international organizations, and twenty-four NGOs. Tim Finch of the National Refugee Welcome Board in the United Kingdom noted, "We wish we had a leader who saw welcoming refugees, not as a chore, but as something to be proud of."

Mike Molloy, adjunct professor at the University of Ottawa, has worked for over thirty-five years in Canadian foreign affairs and the immigration department's refugee branch. He has worked in refugee crises all over the world. He noted, "The government inspired people rather than scared them. The Canadian people were ready. It's a success in terms of political messaging, results, and action. There's no doubt about it." Molloy concluded,

> The magic comes in the way Canadians responded. There is something special about our population. Many of us have refugee and immigration roots. When we see these things happening at such a dramatic scale, we can relate, and there is a willingness to put the time to it. [But] we shouldn't congratulate ourselves. The real question is whether the number of Syrians we've taken in is significant enough to make a difference.

Upon learning of Canada's courageous leadership, I couldn't help but dream about the difference the church could make worldwide. I am certain that many people of faith have participated in Canada's response to the refugees, but there are refugees all over the world that neither Canada nor any other nation can handle on their own. But the church is already in place, able to reach out with love, welcome, and tangibly help anywhere in the world. There is the very real concern of safety in regard to the mission of the church in the world. I'm a husband, father, and grandfather. Of course, I think about safety. But if I live the Love-First creed of Christ, I will follow him and not be ruled by my fears. I am absolutely certain that Jesus would not call me to *more safety* when I could help someone who is *not safe at all.*

More Ready than We Realize

Living the Love-First creed of Christ heals the crisis Christians face in our fellowship and witness, and the world is more ready than we realize. The future is bleak for churches that remain cold toward outsiders and indifferent toward the hurting, no matter where they are from. The next generations are looking for more courage, not more fear—for more tangible compassion, not less concern for the vulnerable. With love restored to its royal position, we become a spring of living water in a world that is parched by racism, discrimination, hate, terrorism and war. And as Jesus already proved in his earthly ministry, the world is more than ready for this elevation of bold and sacrificial love.

But what does this love look like? How do we cleanse ourselves of the counterfeit and fill our hearts, homes, churches, and world with the real thing? This is the next step in our Love-First journey.

Love-First Reflections

- What are some current events that cue us that Christ's universal church is at the threshold of a revolution?
- How might Christ's Love-First creed clash with nationalistic fervor?
- How does it impact our relationships with other Christians, as well as our relationships with others who do not share our faith, if love is not first, both in order and value?
- What are some practical benefits for a Christian, and for a church, that makes the conscious choice to be reshaped by Christ's Love-First creed?
- How is rejecting Love-First also a rejection of the gospel?
- What if Jesus's highest value was personal safety or the safety of those closest to him? How does this relate to the cost of our discipleship? (Meditate on Matthew 10:16–42)

Part 3

THE LOVE-FIRST REVOLUTION

7

THE CORINTHIAN CONDITIONS

If you've been to many weddings, you've probably heard a reading from 1 Corinthians 13. Known as the "Love Chapter," this is perhaps the best-known description of love in ancient literature. But it's no secret to anyone who has even skimmed the rest of the letter to this church in Corinth that the church there was a nightmare. Division, moral decadence, fraud, envy, jealousy, idol worship, slander, and arrogance were their best known characteristics. You could not count on anyone to have your back. And even though the ancient city of Corinth was legendary for its immorality, Paul notes that things were going on in the church that even the pagans would reject. Even the producers for the Jerry Springer Show might have drawn the line with the Corinthian Christians!

Their broken condition was a referendum on their priorities. They were neck deep in religion and ankle deep in love. Their spiritual house was upside down. Their ship of faith had capsized. But why? They prioritized everything above love. The Corinthians were first in sin because they were last in love. To find relief from the mess they were in, they would have to reinvest in love, elevating it to first place, once again learning the conditions that separate the authentic love of God from the counterfeit interaction they called love. *Love-First* love is not an *unconditioned* theological smorgasbord where any definition of love is acceptable. The love of the Corinthians had not been conditioned by Christ, and Paul said this was unacceptable. In fact, he told them that anything they did, and everything they were amounted to a big fat zero. Nothing. Nada. The conditions created by unconditioned love were unacceptable.

First Corinthians 13:1–3 is Paul's "test-of-success" for *love-conditioning*. He outlines six typical markers of a healthy church:

1. We speak God's language.
2. We deliver the prophetic word.
3. We have the inside scoop on God's plan for the world.
4. We know what God thinks about everything.
5. We are missional community-changers with global impact.
6. No risk is too great for the mission.

This reads like a church website "About Us" page. And these six markers are still the identifying marks of a truly Christian church. But then Paul suggests that all this, minus love, looks like this:

1. ______________________________
2. ______________________________
3. ______________________________
4. ______________________________
5. ______________________________
6. ______________________________

Although it stings, Paul's diagnosis is clear: "No matter what I say, what I believe, and what I do, I'm bankrupt without love" (1 Cor. 13:3 THE MESSAGE).Without God-conditioned love, your gifted, bold, theologically brilliant, fearless missional activity gains you nothing and makes you nothing . . . except irritating!

Paul's markers are potential expressions of love, but they are not love. When these things are done without love, then we become like noisy gongs, clanging cymbals, creaking gates, nails on a chalkboard.

Most churches and Christians believe they are great lovers. We believe we are friendly. We believe we are hospitable. We believe our doctrinal genius and missional generosity are proof enough—clear and irrefutable evidence—that we are full of love. The Corinthians were sure they had all knowledge and were on point with God. They were a state-of-the-art church, and their installers were none other than Paul, Peter, and Apollos. But when God is in their house, he notices the L/C—Love Conditioning—isn't working. They have *un*conditioned love, and God is going to move them to condition *their* love, *his* way.

Delusions of Grandeur

Where were they getting all their false confidence? The city of Corinth had a reputation. I often encourage people who are looking to understand the culture of this ancient city to imagine making New Orleans and Atlanta into one city. Corinth had the flavor of a prosperous seaport and the smell of new money. The ancient Greek city was deeply Romanized by the first century, and it swelled with pride, avarice, and depravity. They imagined themselves superior and held sway over the surrounding region with their financial might.

It should come as no surprise that the culture of the city seeped into the culture of the church. The church was in Corinth and Corinth was in the church. In 13:1–4 Paul highlights three of the sources of their deluded grandeur:

1. They were ultra-spiritual.
2. They were known for knowledge.
3. When they gave, it made a big splash.

What deceived them then, is still deceiving us today. Countless times through the years I would hear people describe their spiritual heroes with these glowing terms. Pastors, preachers, professors, and churches are held up as examples to follow without the slightest concern for the authenticity of their love for God and others. Paul's argument is not that these qualities are undesirable or lack potential for great impact, but he is blunt in his assessment of a Christian or church that believes these are sufficient *without* love. He doesn't even offer a grading scale. This is pass/fail. With love, these gifts fill our homes, churches, and neighborhoods with the hope, healing, and happiness God intended for his world. Without love, these are the religious equivalents of trees that bear no fruit and clouds that bring no rain (Jude 1:12).

Are You Ready to Condition Your Love?

I am going to step out on faith and ask you to do some things: First, I'm going to ask you to hang with me while we go through this. If you've come this far, I'm guessing you're in. But second, and more difficult, I'm going to ask you to make some changes—some substantive, tangible, irreversible changes. The stakes have never been higher. As I mentioned in the previous chapter, theologians, anthropologists, sociologists, and historians have been telling us for more than three decades that we are going through the greatest transition in the last five hundred years of Christian history. What you do with this material matters. It matters to your life, your family, your friends, your community, your church, your nation, and your world.

Please hear my heart on this: I do not care if you change your vocabulary. If you want to call God's love *unconditional*, I'm not going to argue the point. But like a voice crying out in the wilderness, I must beg you to live his unconditional love according to his conditions. If we are to end hate before it's too late, we simply can't endure unconditioned love among Christians one more day.

Call it what you want. My desire is more focused: I am advocating for a new generation of believers who will condition their love the way Christ loves us.

Can You Start a Reformation?

Khizr and Ghazala Khan went from virtual obscurity to changing the course of history in six minutes and one second. His brief speech at the Democratic National Convention on July 28, 2016, electrified the nation. He and his wife emigrated from Pakistan in 1980. He completed his law degree at Harvard. They became U.S. citizens and focused on raising their three sons. Khizr loves America and is a staunch supporter of democracy. He wanted to challenge the fear tactic being used in the presidential campaign to paint all Muslims with the same brush. His family is Muslim, they love America, and their middle son was Exhibit A.

Deployed in Iraq with the U.S. army, Captain Humayun Khan died June 8, 2004, protecting his soldiers from a suicide bomber. Everyone who knew Humayun recalled that his life was like his death—always protecting, always serving. Humayun had been active in R.O.T.C., and his parents continued their involvement after his death. For years, Humayun's father was asked to speak at the graduation and swearing-in ceremonies. He spoke proudly of his son's service, but he also told of his son's sacrifice. He wanted each new recruit to take seriously the oath they were making. Being a soldier meant something. There were conditions—real conditions—and his son, with the ultimate sacrifice, embodied them.

We need a generation of Christians who will embody Christ-conditioned love. Loving the world means something to God. His Son is Exhibit A. Being a disciple means something. There are conditions—real conditions—modeled for us by his Son, and we are called to the ultimate sacrifice, to embody them. When we embrace the Love-First creed, our spirituality, knowledge, and resources become powerful tools to bless the world and give others a taste of the good Father who longs to pour his infinite love into their heart.

Trafficking in Christ-Conditioned Love

What does it look like in real life to be reformed into a person of Christ-conditioned love? How does Love-First translate into traffic in Atlanta? If you've been here, 'nuf said. Think *Mad Max*: *Fury Road*, but worse. The film budget was one hundred fifty million dollars. I could have saved them a ton of money with a GoPro camera mounted to the roof of my van in rush-hour traffic.

One afternoon my wife and I were braving the gauntlet. My knuckles were white. My jaw was set. No eye contact with the drivers around me. Lots of hand-waving and yelling. My shoulders were hunched . . . breathing shallow . . . heart racing. A normal drive on Georgia 400. But Susan had had enough. She looked over at me and calmly suggested, "It's a shame these people do not know what a nice person you are." Ouch!

But Susan was right. What in the world was going on with me? Before I started this study, I would have said my problem was a lack of patience, poor anger management, or some other negative spiritual quality. It did not occur to me that the core problem was unconditioned love. I didn't have a patience problem; I had a love problem. All racism is a love problem. Bullying is a love problem. A fit of rage is a love problem. Gossip is a love problem.

All racism is a love problem. Bullying is a love problem. A fit of rage is a love problem. Gossip is a love problem.

The apostle Paul must clarify to the Corinthians—*before he lays out the conditions of love*—that if they take a mechanical approach to the behavior and fail to root everything in love, it will count for absolutely nothing. And worse, it will do even more damage. Many substitute flattery for honor, platitudes for compassion, and attention for affection. They turn worship and salvation into acts and steps, like a punch list on a construction project. They call the singing of hymns, *worship*; the Lord's Supper, *Communion*; having a potluck, *fellowship*; and bowing their heads, *prayer*. I know from my own life that *without* love, these actions are worthless substitutes. Without love, nothing we do in the name of Christ means anything above the clouds or below.

But what about *with* love? When we pursue love first, everything that follows takes on a vibrancy, resiliency, and authenticity that Jesus called the abundant life (John 10:10). This love-conditioned approach to life creates an oasis for souls longing for something real.

This love we long to give is the love we receive. God does not, and will not ever, step outside the conditions he has set for his love. God's love is always everything he promised it would be. It is never a micron less. God never, ever offers a substitute or counterfeit version of his love. His love is never tired. His love is never hypocritical. His love never has a bad day or an off-night. The love of God is marked by the conditions God has set, and it is always one hundred percent pure love. God's love is one hundred percent conditional one hundred percent of the time. And we are the beneficiaries of this love.

Our Creator conditions his love for us. He is our Father who never forgets who he is in the heat of the moment. We are never the unwitting targets of a God who doesn't care to keep it together. And it is this God who is calling us into a culture of love conditioned by the life and teachings of his one and only Son. So if you're ready, or at least you want to be, let's dive into the conditions of the Love-First creed.

Love-First Reflections

- Churches often talk about worship as a set of "acts" (like singing, praying, etc.), and salvation as "steps" (like Step One: Believe, Step Two: Repent, etc.) How does this pattern of structuring our worship and salvation as *acts* and *steps* influence how we think about being in a relationship with God?

- The list below articulates some possible outcomes when the emphasis of our discipleship is directed on what we do rather than who we love. Check the ones you've personally experienced.

  ___ We become excellent performers.
  ___ We rely on the affirmation or praise of others.
  ___ We live like our actions earn us our salvation.
  ___ Results and numbers outweigh people.
  ___ Competition stirs suspicion, jealousy, and division among us.
  ___ We burn out.
  ___ We become more like Jesus.
  ___ The world recognizes we are followers of Jesus.

- The good deeds of any church, *without love*, could be a list titled "All about _________."

  But the same list of good deeds *that are the outgrowth of God's love*, could be more accurately titled, "All about _________."

- Can the world detect between counterfeit love and authentic love? What difference does it make?

8

LOVE IS PATIENT

As Paul begins his famous description of love, this is where he starts. He tells us that Christ-conditioned love is patient. Patience is love-conditioned power. The Corinthians were enamored with power. They loved how the gifts of the Spirit empowered them. These folks were movers of mountains. But Paul knew the difference between conditioned power and *leverage for advantage*. They liked to drop names, create camps of influence in the church, and be on the inside. They liked to use their influence to maintain their status quo and smack down others when they didn't get their way. Rather than serve, they sued. Rather than bless, they cursed. Rather than commune, they consumed. Rather than support, they slandered.

This was their way of justifying getting what they wanted when they wanted it. Instead of following The Way, they were bent on getting their way. But, surprisingly, Paul did not confront them and tell them to be more patient. Rather he reminded them that without love they were nothing: Love is patient. Without Christ-conditioned patience, they gained nothing and they were nothing.

The Corinthians had a reputation of "really being something," so the words of Paul carried a particularly painful sting.

This is true of many churches. Over time we become full of ourselves, and we love being told that we are a "great" church. And there is nothing wrong with giving honor where honor is due and expressing great thanksgiving for all the Lord has done. But if a church believes it is great at love, and yet turns on and off the condition of patience, then we are a creaking gate. We're nails on a chalkboard. We are nothing.

I find this condition especially poignant when I am thinking about how humans relate to one another. Canada's inspiring refugee story caught the attention of European nations while they were in the throes of bitter dissension over the same refugees. In Europe and other parts of the world, patience has grown thin. People are angry. They want this thing solved, and they want answers *now*. But when they were inspired to love, the Canadians found more patience to deal with what one official called "the little bumps and bruises" along the way. Rather than seeing the refugees as a problem to be solved, they saw them as people to be loved. Patience-conditioned love *is* solving the problem for these precious people, and it is changing the hopes and outcomes for baby boys like Alan.

Could it look like this in your church, your community, your family? Maybe you won't sponsor a refugee family, but America is full of "relational refugees." Our contentious bickering, political bantering, racial slandering, and economic idolatry have created a more divided nation than I have seen in my lifetime. How can we make a real, lasting difference in unifying the social fabric of our land? I believe it begins with conditional love—the Christ-conditioned love *with* which we are lavishly blessed, and *to* which we submit our lives.

Let me encourage you with a special story about two women and a preacher growing in patience-conditioned love.

The Preacher and the Purse

It was not easy to accept that our church struggled with racism. It was hard for us to humble ourselves enough to admit it. And since most of us were white in 1998 (95 percent), it was pretty easy to convince ourselves that we were on top of the race issue. After all, who was going to challenge us?

But the Holy Spirit wouldn't leave this alone. He went to work in our hearts, and we began the intentional journey toward answering Jesus's prayer, "Thy kingdom come, thy will be done, *on earth as it is in heaven*"(Matt. 6:10). To get a glimpse of what God's people look like when they are gathered in heaven, check out Revelation 7:9–14.

Our path forward included openly teaching about racism and confronting our biases with the teachings of Scripture. The Bible is packed with verses that blow up ethnic supremacy, segregation that benefits one race above another, and cultural privilege. So my co-worker and friend, Ken Snell, and I were teaching this series on Wednesday evenings. As the weeks went by, some members became more considerate about their biases and prejudices, while others became more visibly angry.

Following the class one evening, I did not realize that a member of the class had been waiting to talk with me after almost everyone else had left. I walked through a door into the lobby and, out of nowhere, she whacked me in the side of the head with her purse. As you can imagine, I was stunned in more ways than one. My glasses were somewhere on the floor, mixed in with her lipstick, pocketbook, and other things that hide away in women's handbags. As I was trying to fit my glasses back on my face, she lit into me again, only this time verbally. "People like you are the problem," she yelled, while stabbing me in the chest with her index finger. "There is no problem until people like you stir the pot. You're talking about the Old South. This is the New South. And the only reason anyone gets upset is because people like you bring up the past!"

She seemed mad as a hornet, but it turned out she was scared, hurt, and her pride was bruised. I will admit, I was not too happy either, but the Holy Spirit gave us some much-needed help. I replied, "I know you're upset, and I am not sure what the solution is. But I don't believe this is the best way to end our evening. Can we sit down and at least pray together?" One of our African-American sisters joined us for prayer and conversation. She shared experiences and concerns that white citizens in our community almost never think about. It was eye-opening and heart softening. Transparency coupled with empathy led to tears and embrace.

My friend Jerry Morgan calls this *The Change Moment*. He writes about Jesus's restoring Peter (as recorded in John 21):

> Maybe I am reading too much into this conversation, but I think what is happening is that Peter, maybe for the first time, is being totally honest with his Lord. It would have been so easy for Peter to say, yes, Lord, I agape (love) you, but finally Peter realizes, I can't fool this Jesus, never could, so I might as well just be honest about where I am in this relationship. Besides, Peter's lack of honesty is what got Peter into this mess.[1]

As I watched these two sisters in our church "get honest" with each other, I was deeply moved by their patience. Neither reached for their power, yet both were empowered to share truth. This is the hidden secret of godly patience: the patient are positioned in power—*the power to do good.*

In each New Testament text where patience is commended, it is over and against the destructiveness of unconditioned expressions of power. The apostle Paul tells the Galatian Christians that their hatred, their fits of rage, and their dissension are going to tear them apart. The destructive attitudes and actions Paul lists are all ungodly attempts to express power.

But why? Why would brothers and sisters in Christ, family members, or citizens of the same community and nation treat each other this way? We might be responding to our wounds, our upbringing, our neurological wiring, an illness, pressures in another part of life, an overwhelming sense of responsibility, the desire to "fix" things, or the fact that we want our way and have an overblown estimate of our opinions. Whatever is driving our impatience, every life in our circle of influence would improve if we would embrace the patience-conditioned love of Christ.

But if we do decide to make a change, what will happen to us? Will we get run over by those who have no interest in patience? These are very real concerns. Left unexamined, these concerns will poison our willingness to internalize the Love-First creed of Christ.

Insecurity and pride can look like twins. Sometimes when a person is coming across as arrogant, bossy, and demanding, it is a response to their insecurity. Put another way, *it is a display of power to mask their fear of powerlessness.* The Galatians, like the Corinthians, chose to put others down as a way of building themselves up, and it wasn't working in either church. Paul offered a solution: the Christ-creed of love: "Serve each other with love. The whole law is made complete in this one command: '*Love your neighbor as you love yourself.*' If you go on hurting each other and tearing each other apart, be careful, or you will completely destroy each other" (Gal. 5:13b–15 NCV).

Insecurity and pride can look like twins. Sometimes when a person is coming across as arrogant, bossy, and demanding, it is a response to their insecurity. Put another way, *it is a display of power to mask their fear of powerlessness.*

Paul knew better than to leave them to their own unconditioned definition of love. This life they were called to live was defined, infused, and empowered by the Holy Spirit. Their relationships were to be conditioned by "love, joy, peace, *patience*, kindness, goodness, faithfulness, gentleness, and self-control" (5:22–23a). Paul closed with a final warning that those who abandoned these conditions would find themselves in an endless cycle of conceit, provocation, and jealousy.

Is patience a consistent condition of your love? It is hard for others to feel loved when patience is not one of your conditions. Although the "night of the purse attack" worked out, most of us would not be in favor of others regularly expressing their "love" to us that way. I have heard people use the time-honored wording, "I love my ___________ (insert children, spouse, church, or whomever) unconditionally." I think they mean "without limit," or "I will always love them no matter what." Sound familiar? This is what we normally call unconditional love. But it is that *un*conditional part that is battering, bruising, and busting our relationships.

I have to remind you, I'm not trying to change your vocabulary. I am advocating *Christ-conditioned* love: love that is conditioned by the qualities that make God's love amazing. I am pressing this point because the fabric of our churches, families, and society is being torn apart by *un*conditioned love—love that is not held to the high standards of God's conditions.

What would it be like if every Christian you know, including you, submitted to a complete overhaul of love, no longer accepting the low bar of worldly love, but accepting nothing less than the high bar of God's love? We often express in our worship, liturgy, sermons, and especially Communion that "it was not the nails that held Jesus to the cross, but his love for his Father and his love for us." I believe this confession, and I also believe that it is right to hold up Jesus as our standard. If this is the case, then we must acknowledge the plain implication of Jesus's example. Under the absolute worst of circumstances, Jesus did not avenge himself. Rather than reacting to their taunts, trash talk, and torture, he restrained his power. Though ten thousand angels were poised for an extraction and destruction mission (Matt. 26:53), Jesus modeled patience-conditioned love.

His example from the cross is both persuasive and pragmatic: Offer your pain to God, forgive those who are causing the pain, admit your physical limitations, make a difference where you can right now, put everything in the hands of God, and be confident when you've done what he called you to do. At Calvary, patience-conditioned love was on full display. Jesus remained fully engaged in God's will for him until he could boldly proclaim, "It is finished."

Love-First Reflections

First, some questions to consider as we try to condition our love with patience.

- Where in our society right now could you see patience-conditioned love making the greatest difference?

- Where are you, what are you doing, or who are you with when you have the most difficult time holding to the love condition of restraining your power instead of avenging yourself?

- What role does social-media and instantaneous news play in our struggle to respond to people and circumstances with patience?

- How are local and national leaders tempted to abandon patience when confronted with questions and crises? How does their patience or lack of patience affect our interaction with other people, especially those who have a differing opinion?

- Write a prayer that will confirm this component of Christ-conditioned love in your daily life and interactions. (For this and future chapters, I want to suggest that you write a prayer that will help you, and one that highlights the challenges you are facing.)

Now consider a possible prayer that highlights the problem you are committed to face.

> Dear God,
>
> People who do not agree with me on politics, religion, and which way to load toilet paper make me mad. I have decided to abandon patience with them, but I'm going to need your help. I want to insult them with the most impact. I want to paint them as stupid and inept to the largest audience that will listen. I don't want anyone disagreeing with me, telling me I'm wrong, or suggesting that I should be more patient, listen more, or anything like that. I know you are not normally on board with this kind of behavior, and it doesn't really follow the Love-First creed of Jesus, but I'm up to here with this nonsense. I'm not going to let anyone, including you, make me slow down and consider my actions, my witness, or most of all Scripture. Please promise me that you will be good with

this, and let Jesus and the Holy Spirit also know so that they won't try to interfere. Uh . . . In Jesus's name. Amen.

Okay, I realize that none of us would really want to word a prayer that way. But consider why I do this (and yes, I do this exercise). When I write out my thoughts, motives, and potential actions, it makes them more real to me. It exposes the darkness and shows me my sin. It allows me to see how I am behaving, and it breaks my heart before the God who so graciously loves me.

Now consider instead a prayer that can really help.

Dear Father,

I depend on you to keep every condition of your perfect love, *all* the time and *every* time. I depend on you to be patient with me beyond all measure. It would seem so hypocritical to freely receive your unlimited, patience-conditioned love and then turn around and run my mouth or put others down. I pray, Father, that the words of my mouth and the meditations of my heart will be acceptable in your sight, O, Lord, my Rock and my Redeemer. I commit to the conditions of your love, and pray for the strength and courage to hold to your condition of patient love in every relationship and circumstance. For those I have already wounded, bless me today as I reach out and apologize. Prepare me in advance to love them patiently if they do not receive my apology right away. And for those who may experience my impatience today, please alert me in the moment and soften my heart with your love to quickly and humbly apologize. I pray this in Jesus's Name. Amen.

I encourage you to do this same exercise for the following chapters. This can make an important, and perhaps difficult exercise truly transformational.

9
LOVE IS KIND

Our first granddaughter was born in Yekaterinburg, Russia, while our son and daughter-in-law were serving with a church-planting team. Susan and I read to her over Skype, but our arms ached to hold her. We departed for Russia with love bubbling over. Our first layover was in New York, where the whole world seems to gather. We were on a moving walkway packed with people, standing behind an elderly couple arriving from France. As they reached the end of the walkway, they stumbled and both of them fell in a heap. People just kept coming like packages on a conveyor belt as Susan and I tried to help this couple to their feet and out of the way.

Now I'm not indicting *every* New Yorker with this incident, but a dude wearing a Yankees ball cap and jacket yelled at the couple and at us, "Get the (expletive) out of the way!" He clumsily stepped *through* us to dramatize his frustration. With bags and body swinging about, he nearly knocked Susan and me to the floor.

All who know my wife understand why I affectionately call her "velvet titanium," and now this New Yorker was about to experience the titanium. With the French couple now standing and stable, Susan marched after this guy, and I knew where she was going. When she caught the scurrying ruffian, she reached out (yes!) and tapped him on the shoulder. He tried to sluff her off, but she wasn't having it. She delivered an exquisitely incisive thirty-second monologue on kindness that he is likely never to forget. As a mother of grown children, she was able to address him as such, especially since he had acted like one (a fact that was also communicated!). She left him with a warning that in the future "he had better treat others as he would like to be treated." I'm not sure if his gait was normally a gallop, but I am certain he made his gate with plenty of time to consider her assessment of his behavior. That's my girl!

But was she kind? Were they just alike—Susan and the New Yorker—two faces of unkindness? Kindness, like patience, will require some definition. My friend Patrick almost died from overdosing. He knows the terrible torment and deadening darkness of addiction, and he also knows the overwhelming power of Jesus who can deliver on his promise of full redemption. Patrick has a way of communicating in recovery meetings that cuts to the heart of where many people find themselves. He will often say, "Don't mistake my kindness for weakness." Patrick realizes that kindness and strength are not at odds with each other. Boldness does not have to bow out for kindness to enter. Susan was kind to challenge the unkindness of the traveler in New York because she did not seek her own good, but his.

My men's Bible study group studied kindness together. One of the surprising "aha" moments for me was how much strength is required to be kind! One of our leaders, Scott Gage, calls kindness the "workhorse of love."

More Than Howdy and Bless Your Heart

Many people measure kindness with social comfortability. If someone says and does things that help us feel welcome and respected, we see them as kind. I have learned this can be skin deep, or even a mindless greeting with no substance when real needs arise.

Kindness in the language of Paul's day implied goodness, generous, gentle, useful; a mellowing of all that would be harsh; active dealings with others involving equity and justice. It is a grace that pervades the whole nature. In Greek literature, this word was often coupled with philanthropy, the benevolent and active love of your fellow humans. The All-Pro Dad ministry calls kindness the "unsung hero in all relationships." The ancient Jews held this character trait in the highest regard:

> Whoever is kind to the poor lends to the LORD, and he will reward them for what they have done. (Prov. 19:17)

> Whoever oppresses the poor shows contempt for their Maker, but whoever is kind to the needy honors God. (Prov. 14:31)

Scottish biologist and evangelist Henry Drummond was deeply convicted about the role of kindness in all aspects of life. In his treatise on love, Drummond quoted a familiar saying, "The greatest thing a man can do for his heavenly Father is to be kind to some of his other children."[1]

God is kind. Kindness pervades every aspect of his character while compromising none. As evidenced in his message to and through Hosea, God can call his people to accountability, rebuke them for their waywardness, and exude his kindness as naturally as we exhale breath. "I led them with cords of human kindness, with ties of love," God says in Hosea 11:4. "To them I was like one who lifts a little child to the cheek, and I bent down to feed them."

This same theme flows into the New Testament descriptions of God. Hear Jesus, for example, when he says, "Love your enemies, do good to them, and lend to them without expecting to get anything back. Then your reward will be great, and you will be children of the Most High, *because he is kind to the ungrateful and wicked*. Be merciful, just as your Father is merciful" (Luke 6:35–36, emphasis mine). Not only is our character displayed in the natural inclinations to make love a transaction that ultimately benefits self, but we are also compared with God who would have every right for such a self-absorbed track, yet refuses it. God's love is conditional, and even the ungrateful and wicked cannot lure him into the *un*conditioned life. And the teachings of Jesus only serve to reinforce the fact that not just any definition of love is orthodox. The Christ-creed of Love-First is conditioned by kindness, and there is no loophole, including ingratitude or wickedness. How can this be?

My parents started a construction company when I was two years old. They both worked long hours. Our house, offices, shop, and construction yard were eventually all on the same land, so there wasn't much separation between family life and business. Dump trucks, backhoes, and bulldozers were our life. One afternoon in my late teens I saw a man drive up and park his car in front of the office. Dad came out and after they talked for a few minutes the man opened his trunk and pulled out what looked like a shotgun and a couple of hunting rifles. He handed them to my dad, closed his trunk, they shook hands, and he got in his car and drove away.

The whole thing seemed a little out of place. I followed my dad into his office, where he put the guns in the corner. I asked him what that was all about. He told me that the man had owed him some money for quite some time but was unable to pay the debt, so dad received the guns in place of payment. I reminded him that he already had a shotgun and hunting rifles, so this didn't make sense. At this my dad shared something that has stuck with me until this day: "Always give a man a dignified way to move forward."

I realized that it wasn't about the guns. Dad offered the man a way to retain his dignity. You might think, well, why didn't he just cancel the debt altogether? But that is the thing about kindness, it isn't about your feeling better about yourself; but rather, it is about doing what is good, useful, and beneficial for someone else. Kindness to this man was for him to be able to "pay his debt" and maintain his dignity.

Kind Like Jesus

The apostle Paul tells us to "clothe ourselves with kindness" as we put on the new self in Christ (Col. 3:12). The kindness and compassion expected in our relationships with one another are built on and measured by the kindness we receive from Christ. It is the kindness of God that melts our hardened hearts and opens our ears to his call to repentance (Rom. 2:4). It is the kindness of God our Savior that appears and brings us salvation (Tit. 3:4–8).

You already may be familiar with these passages, but there are more. Notice, for example, how the apostle Paul alludes to a fuller meaning of kindness:

> But because of his great love for us, God, who is rich in mercy, made us alive with Christ even when we were dead in transgressions—it is by grace you have been saved. And God raised us up with Christ and seated us with him in the heavenly realms in Christ Jesus, in order that in the coming ages he might show the incomparable riches of his grace, expressed in his kindness to us in Christ Jesus. (Eph. 2:4–7)

How is God expressing his kindness to us in Christ Jesus? Could this guide us in how to live kindness-conditioned love toward each other and the world around us?

The following passage uses the same Greek word for kindness, but the English word used in the translation is different. "Rid yourselves of all malice and all deceit, hypocrisy, envy, and slander of every kind. Like newborn babies, crave pure spiritual milk, so that by it you may grow up in your salvation, now that you have tasted that the Lord is *good*" (1 Pet. 2:1–3, emphasis mine).

The New Living Translation uses "kindness" in place of the word "good" in the NIV reading above. Most translations maintain the word "good," because it is a familiar quote of Psalm 34:8. The Greek translation of the Old Testament also has the same Greek word translated "kindness," and the lexicons give room for this breadth of meaning. But there is a greater lesson for us in these verses than learning which English word is best. Notice the transformational nature of experiencing the kindness of the Lord. The call to rid ourselves of malice, deceit, hypocrisy, envy, and slander of every kind is rooted in our personal experience of God's kindness.

The theology here is important. The Christ-creed is Love-First. Love is above all virtues (Col. 3:14), but it is also before all other thoughts, motives, and actions. God's love precedes everything. We love because he first loved us. Let's take another step in the orthodoxy of the Christ-creed. The apostle Paul writes of Christ's Love-First creed in some of Scripture's most unforgettable words:

> You see, at just the right time, when we were *still powerless*, Christ died for the *ungodly*. Very rarely will anyone die for a righteous person, though for a good person someone might possibly dare to die. But God demonstrates his own love for us in this: *While we were still sinners*, Christ died for us.
>
> Since we have now been justified by his blood, how much more shall we be saved from God's wrath through him! For if, *while we were God's enemies*, we were reconciled to him through the death of his Son, how much more, having been reconciled, shall we be saved through his life! Not only is this so, but we also boast in God through our Lord Jesus Christ, through whom we have now received reconciliation. (Rom. 5:6–11, emphasis mine)

There is no way to miss the point. Four times, using different words, Paul drives home the point that God allowed us to "taste and see" that he is good (kind) before we did anything that deserved it or even indicated interest in him and his Kingdom. This is the message of Jesus in Luke 6:27–36. The kindness of God is tasted because God is kind to the ungrateful, wicked, powerless, ungodly, sinning, enemies, and so on.

Uh-oh. Is this where the kindness-condition is headed? Yes. In fact, it is like kindness-squared. Not only does the kindness of God call us to rid ourselves of our ungratefulness, wickedness, malice, deceit, hypocrisy, envy, and every kind of slander, we are then called to be kind to people who still retain all of these nasty characteristics. When Jesus calls us to love our enemies, he is speaking first out of his experience with us—you and me! We recoil from this because we don't think we have ever been that bad. I'm not arguing that point. We are not his enemies because we are *that* bad, but because he is *that* good.

He could not help but be our enemy, any more than a white blood cell can make an alliance with an infection. God had to be kind toward his enemies to save those he already loved. We love because he *first* loved us. When we are called into the Love-First creed, we are being called to kindness-conditioned love—the love that puts a target on every enemy, at which we then aim the kindness we have received.

God came into our midst, became flesh, and experienced the full wrath of our enmity toward him. God did not cleanse us before he joined us. Without compromising his holiness he wrapped himself in complete humanness. Not a day of his ministry went by without his being reminded of the great gap he came to heal. His life was threatened over and over. He was blasphemed, cursed, and slandered. Those who should have known him first were the ones who hated him most.

And yet he could not unhook from the conditions he set for his love. He wept over Jerusalem, longing to gather the people in the safety and warmth of his love, but they only hated him all the more. He was despised and rejected. The religious folks who knew everything sat around in their small groups and reviled him, persecuted him, and said all manner of evil against him falsely. But where did this leave him? After thirty-three years in the flesh, and a thousand days of grinding ministry, he could have said in his heart, "To the pit of hell with all of you!" He *could* have, but here are the words he actually said: "Come to me, all you who are weary and burdened, and I will give you rest. Take my yoke upon you and learn from me, for I am gentle and humble in heart, and you will find rest for your souls. For my yoke is *easy* and my burden is light" (Matt. 11:28–30, emphasis mine).

Does it shock you to learn that our word for "kindness" is translated "easy." Jesus says, "Listen, I know your life is tough. There are visible and invisible problems and pressures that wear you out. You feel like you are crumbling beneath your load. You still have the energy to give me a hard time, and you use the strength I give you to sin against me. So where does that leave me toward you?" Read his words again . . . slowly.

> Come to me.
> I will give you rest.
> Take my yoke (my conditions) upon you and learn from me.
> For I am gentle and humble in heart.
> And you will find rest for your souls.
> For my yoke is kind
> And my burden is light.

Can we trust that far beyond whatever we are gaining from our malice, deceit, underhandedness, envy, and slander, the *yoke* (the conditioned-life) he is offering will bless us infinitely more?

Proverbs 11:17 says, "Those who are kind benefit themselves, but the cruel bring ruin on themselves."

Just to clarify: Jesus does invite us to take his yoke upon ourselves—his constraint, his reign, his control, his conditions—and learn from him. But he unequivocally testifies that his conditions are easy (kind) and his burden is light. So how can a constraint, a set of mandatory conditions make life easier? Kinder? I actually looked up the synonyms for "yoke," and not one of them looked good. (Oppression, burden, bondage, encumbrance, drag, load, annoyance, repression.) These are depressing. But none of these serve as the descriptor for Jesus; he chooses "kind."

The best choice from the lexical list to explain how Jesus is using the yoke metaphor may be the word "useful." Jesus implies that allowing his "burden" to become the conditions we trust in our relationships will prove useful, good, kind . . . and easy. Consider the following four-point description of the work of kindness in our relationships.[2]

1. Kindness Provides a Shared Foundation

Chemistry may bring us together, but kindness is the key to growing together. My wife and I are both strong-willed people. We enjoy this component of our marriage now, but it was difficult in the beginning because we lacked the maturity to strongly disagree *and* be kind. One evening after an inappropriate argument, my wife saw our young daughter in her bedroom praying. When Susan asked what she was praying about, Amy admitted that she was praying that we would treat each other better. We had given ourselves permission to abandon kindness when our frustration with each other overinflated. But that was it. That night was the change-moment for us both. We consciously committed to never speak to each other again with those words, that tone, or an elevated volume. The kindness-condition became a non-negotiable.

After this change took root in our home, I became more cognizant of the destruction caused by "social bullies" whose posture, tone of voice, choice of words, facial expressions, and body language all threaten reprisal if you disagree with their conclusions or statements. Like me, they are blind to the impact of their social bullying. The strength of their opinion, their sense of responsibility to "set others straight" (at least according to their assessment of things) is so strong that they believe their behavior is justified. All of our relationships will be upgraded and our influence will be expanded when we ask the Holy Spirit to change the tone of our voice and our facial expressions to more fully reflect the heart of a person who sees the just and fair treatment of others as a genuine expression of kindness (Jeremiah 9:24).

2. Kindness Heals Hurts

Relationships bring us into close enough proximity with each other to create some blessed encounters, but also some bruised egos. My dad was crisp and concise when I asked him, "Why do relationships seem to cause pain?" His reply, "Because humans do things." Yes, that was his answer, and I'm smiling and shaking my head as I did the first time he said it. His point is simple: if you want to get close to another human, you are inviting help and hurt, fun and frustration, compliments and complaints, their best and worst behavior. It is just the way humans are. When we love each other, we do our best to elevate and normalize good behavior while minimizing and eliminating bad behavior, but it's never perfect. Hurts happen and kindness heals.

3. Kindness Takes Away the Rough Edges of Disagreement

We often find ourselves abandoning kindness in increments. We may begin a conversation well but then "lose it" when faced with disagreement or even disrespect. My friend Mike Thornton says that "a disagreement done kindly is a discussion." In our home, we practice five phrases to keep the stream of kindness flowing:

- "I didn't mean to say that, can I please begin again?"
- "That was an overstatement. What I mean to say is . . ."
- "I am not as ready for this conversation as I thought I was. Can I please take a step back and come back to this when I am more of who I need to be?"
- "I don't think I am as ready as you are to have this conversation. Are you okay if I listen and do not respond? I don't have confidence that I will be who I know I need to be."
- "Tell me more . . ." (and ten more versions of that simple phrase!).

4. Kindness Is Not Just about the Other Person, It Is about Us

Loving kindness is a character condition of the Christ-follower. We are kind to others out of our faithfulness to our calling. While others will greatly enjoy and appreciate your consistent kindness, your kindness will not really be tested until someone treats you unkindly.

The greatest competition for an elite athlete is their own past performance. Some Olympians already hold world records, yet they seek to improve their marks to even higher standards. They are already the best in the world, so their drive must come from an internal commitment to conditioning.

Jesus Christ is the world record holder for holiness, the Olympian of sinlessness, the champion of kindness. But humans set the bar so low he really had no external competition. Even his own detractors, trying to trap him, tapped into his impeccable, flawless reputation, as in Luke 20:21: "Teacher, we know that you speak and teach what is right, and that you do not show partiality but teach the way of God in accordance with the truth."

Consider the benefits of embracing world-class kindness. You will be more like God. You will demonstrate Christ through your life. You will not grieve the Spirit. You will be a great witness for Jesus. As Frederick William Faber said, "Kindness has converted more sinners than zeal, eloquence, or learning." You will have less shame from negative interactions. Like the young man in the New York airport, you may have a reputation as a "social bully." By your lack of kindness you've earned a negative reputation. Kindness can turn this around where others see you as someone who is safe and can be trusted.

King Solomon wrote nearly three millennia ago, "Love and faithfulness keep a king safe, through love his throne is made secure" (Prov. 20:28). Kind people uphold the dignity of others. Kind people help the fallen. Kind people call the unkind to help, not hurt. Kindness is concrete action. When others remember us, *and consider Jesus because of us*, let our overwhelming kindness and attentiveness to the needs of others be first in their minds!

Love-First Reflections

- How have the wounds you have experienced in life influenced you to be more kind to others, or less kind?
- What are the circumstances where you have built a reputation of kindness, and are there some who would not characterize you as kind?
- Which relationships in your life present a real challenge to your kindness, and what will you do to develop a more noticeable and consistent kindness in these relationships?

- Kindness is a condition of life, an attitude of the mind, and a disposition of our affections. It costs no money, but this doesn't mean it's cheap. Kindness can be expressed in every interaction. Our kindness toward others initiates inexhaustible ripples of grace and healing that only God in heaven can track. How will you start a ripple of kindness today?

LOVE IS NOT ENVIOUS

In Paul's profile of divine love, the "love is" section has only two conditions while his "love is not" section has eight! I'm not sure if every church needs so extensive a list, but most of the negative qualities he discusses reflect the behavior he's been confronting throughout the letter. The irony is that they actually need anyone to point out that these traits are bad for love! The Corinthians were definitely envious, boastful, puffed up, rude, self-seeking, short-fused, and unforgiving. As is often the case with our shortcomings, there are still valuable lessons to be learned.

I googled, "How to become more envious," and all that came up was "how to *overcome* envy and jealousy." My next search was, "More boastful?" The results gave me sites on "how to deal with boastful people," and "how to make sure *you* are not coming across boastful." Pride? You guessed it. The sites either taught how to be confident without being prideful, or how to be proud of your accomplishments without being "cocky or conceited." You see the trend. I searched all eight items on Paul's *love-is-not* list. Most websites that are devoted to encouraging and equipping people away from these disturbing qualities are *not* Christian. People just know this list of eight is bad for you and for those around you.

My gastroenterologist is a genius diagnostician and gets straight to the point. Her medical training at Emory, Duke, and Johns Hopkins certainly gives her an edge, but she is undeniably gifted. We met in September 2007 after I collapsed in my driveway on a Saturday morning. I was losing blood, and it was somehow related to my history of gastro-related issues. After getting me patched up and out of the hospital, she set out to solve my health issues.

I arrived ahead of schedule for the follow-up appointment. Her office staff did all the typical prep work, including dressing me in what I call the "insurance gown" (because it only makes you think you're covered)! She came into the exam room and hit me with her list of questions. I was reciting my health history, including what different doctors had told me along the way. When she disapproved, she would stop me and say something like, "So the doctor told you that? Well, he was completely wrong. The human body does not function like that. Next."

Whoa! No professional courtesy there. It took me a while to realize that she wasn't proud, boastful, rude, or self-seeking. She's about the business of healing, and her gift is diagnosis. When my symptoms and the other doctor's conclusions did not add up, she didn't waste time entertaining false possibilities.

Paul's List of Eight

Paul is acting like a physician in 1 Corinthians 13. The patient is terribly sick but has been unwilling to accept Paul's diagnosis. So he is articulating the exact conditions of their illness. In essence he is saying, "*Healthy* Christians do not have these symptoms. When you have any of these eight symptoms, you are sick." Let's take the time to accurately define these symptoms so that we can diagnose them.

With each symptom, I want to begin Paul's definition with one word, "Healthy." I want us to know the difference between healthy love and diseased love. So let's get to the "love is not" conditions.

Healthy Love Is Not Envious

Kirby and Jeff had been buddies since they were three years old. I met them and our friendship began to grow in our early twenties. They were super athletes, great musicians, funny, popular, and talented. Our friendship grew and we began creating memories, but there was a problem, and it had to be addressed. About a dozen of us met nearly every Tuesday morning at our house for a guys' Bible study, but one week in early December 1986 Kirby and Jeff showed up by themselves. When I asked them where the rest of the guys were, Kirby said, "We told them not to come because we needed to talk some things over with you."

My heart was in my throat. It's never fun to be confronted, and I wasn't sure what it was about. I was insecure and afraid.

Kirby started out, "We could be a lot better friends if you would let us."

Ugh! I knew it. I had already wrecked quite a few friendships with my insecurities, and I was on the verge of losing two I treasured. What could I say? How could I smooth this over? My mind was racing, spinning, trying to manipulate an outcome. And then it all just came grinding to a halt. You see, I knew what the problem was. It wasn't a mystery, I just didn't want to confess it . . . but I did.

"I'm jealous," I said plainly. "I am jealous of you both. You are all the things I am not. You are gifted athletes, popular, funny, and talented at everything you do. And I am none of those things. You've known each other your whole lives, so when you go somewhere, like fishing on Lake Seneca, I get jealous, and then I pout. Yes. I pout. I lie about what's wrong. I say, 'I'm fine,' or 'I'm tired,' but that's not true. I am pouting because I am jealous."

Now I want to clarify something for my readers: this is not a hypothetical situation or a summary of my statement. This is what I said. I want you to know this, because it was the first time I ever "got real" like that. I have to admit that telling two other grown men that you are jealous is like throwing up on yourself in public! I felt like a junior high student. And the word "pout" is no upgrade! I felt completely exposed, vulnerable, *and honest*. In spite of how awful it felt for those stinking words to come out of my mouth, it was incredible. I had never felt so empowered and free.

They both looked a little stunned, but without missing a beat Jeff looked at me and said, "Did it ever dawn on you that if we only wanted friends like us, we already had each other?"

I couldn't believe what he was saying. His words meant that they liked me more than I liked me. No, they loved me.

My mind was racing again, but spinning in a new direction. Could it be that I didn't have to feel this way about myself, or others?

My wife was "hovering" in the kitchen so that she could listen in without looking like she was listening in. I looked up at her silhouette and thought, "Then maybe she really does love me the way she says she does." The Holy Spirit seized the moment to open up my heart to God. I was determined not to shed a tear in front of my buddies, but my heart nearly exploded when I realized that God truly loves me the way he promises he does.

My life was changed. Jealousy was pounded into the ground like a tent peg. James 5:16 describes what happened to me that day: "Confess your sins to each other and pray for each other so that you may be healed. The prayer of a righteous person is powerful and effective." Whatever you believe this verse promises about restoring health, it begins with confession of sin. When I named my sin—no dancing around it to make it something it wasn't—I found healing.

In our church family we treasure diversity, and the multiplicity of skin color can actually overshadow other ways we experience life differently. One of our African-American elders noted to me that "economic diversity can be as much or more contentious and difficult to work through than ethnicity or skin color." This came to the forefront in March 2014 when we offered our first "Hospitality Challenge."

The whole idea of hospitality in Scripture is to love the "other," the person you do not know, or who does not appear to be like you. The Greek word translated hospitality is *philoxenia*, "love strangers." In our church we are learning the difference between diversity and integration. We had to get to know each other. So we challenged every member of our church to have a meal in the home of another member in the month of March. Thirty-one days to have one meal in the home, no restaurants allowed. We were going to get into each other's space.

You would have thought I had denied the virgin birth! The cacophony of lament rising up from the church was so surprising. The tsunami of complaints were boiled down to three main waves:

1. "My schedule is already so full I'm at my breaking point. I can't add one thing more."
2. "I don't have time to get my house cleaned and presentable for guests."
3. "I don't feel comfortable having people over. I feel uneasy."

I have to admit that I was taken aback. But as I listened, I thought, "Satan is trying to hold back the growth of love in this church. This is an attack of the enemy to keep us love-sick."

After prayer and discussion with our elders, I addressed the church in a sermon. I noted that if our schedules are so crammed full of activity that we cannot find two hours out of the 744 hours in March to spend time with a member of our church family, we are sick. This is a symptom of spiritual disease. Since I was on a roll, I continued. "If you cannot shovel a path from the front door to your dining room table sometime this month to show hospitality to another member of this church family, you are sick." As you can imagine, everyone was loving this sermon, so I capped it off with, "I believe we are struggling with envy, jealousy, and covetousness. We are worried that people with more will look down on our home, or that people with large houses will feel judged when someone comes for dinner. These are spiritual diseases that create sin-sickness in our souls."

Rather than the church covering their ears, rushing the pulpit, and drowning me in the baptistry, we all began to realize the truth. We were able to mutually confess that we were battling these potentially terminal illnesses. But where do we go to find healing? I shared with the church that day another finding from the original Greek text of Scripture: *hospitality* and *hospital* share the same root. Hospitality could heal us if we were willing to let go of our envy.

Hospitality and *hospital* share the same root. Hospitality could heal us if we were willing to let go of our envy.

Now although we got off to a slow start, the month turned into one long party of fellowship. Instagram, Facebook, and Twitter became a social-media photo album of our growing love. Some families who did not speak the same language invited friends who were bilingual to create bridges of love. We were not even to the end before another cry arose from the members, "We have to do this again!" We have done it two more times as a church, but it changed us. People not only became more active in spending time with each other, but envy lost its grip. Healthy love replaced the love-sickness that had plagued us.

Well, back to Kirby and Jeff. That night in December 1986 changed my future. From that time on I noticed that I enjoyed people more. I cheered for athletes without looking for their Achilles heel, or without having to find some negative point to make them look bad in the eyes of others. I began to enjoy the musicians in my life, the brainiacs, the titans in business that I met. I was being shaped for a future where I would lead Bible studies with pro athletes, millionaires, heads of universities, and CEOs of world-recognized corporations. God granted me the opportunity to meet and serve alongside icons in our nation's civil rights movement. I believe the defeat of jealousy and envy opened the door for me to see people—wonderful, valuable, normal people—in and through their gifts, talents, and accomplishments. I didn't have to worry about how much better they were at everything because they weren't going to decide whether or not they would accept or like me based on my ability to do the things they did.

This shift also saved my ministry. It became apparent early on in ministry that others in our church, no matter which church, were going to be more talented and gifted than I was. On any given Sunday I was never going to be the best speaker, preacher, or teacher in the sanctuary. I didn't have to worry any longer about being the smartest theologian or the best-read member of our church or leadership team. I was free to be me and free to love you. I was free.

Paul doesn't pull this list out of the hat. The love conditions in 1 Corinthians 13 take direct aim toward their *un*conditioned love in the Corinthian church. The church is suffocating in rivalry. Paul blames the divisions among them directly on their lack of orthodoxy—their failure to teach and hold to the faithful teachings of Christ and Scripture. But what command are they breaking? What orthodoxy have they compromised to put themselves in the ditch?

> Brothers and sisters, I could not address you as people who live by the Spirit but as people who are still worldly. . . . For since there is jealousy and quarreling among you, are you not worldly? Are you not acting like mere humans? For when one says, "I follow Paul," and

> another, "I follow Apollos," are you not mere human beings? (1 Cor. 3:1–4)

In my decades of ministry I have heard members and leaders of churches over and over lay the blame for division or relational strain on doctrine. In my inexperience, I would disagree with them. I would even quote Christian scholars and sages who would lay the true blame for divisiveness on immaturity and worldly attitudes.

I'm going on record with this confession: I was wrong. The keepers of orthodoxy *were right* all along. Every division that has ever happened in the church, locally or globally, has been rooted in doctrine. And it is correct to lay the blame for these divisions on those who drifted from the truth—for whatever reason—and exchanged it for a lie. But what is the lie? Which doctrine did they ditch that led to the division? Which cropped creed was the culprit?

The commandment they no longer held with immovable reverence was the Love-First creed of Christ. For them, the first and greatest command was nothing but a footnote. Their love, no longer Christ-conditioned, was now full of envy. Both James and Paul issued warnings to their first-century audiences about the destructiveness of envy, but everything they wrote applies to me as well:

> Who is wise and understanding among you? Let them show it by their good life, by deeds done in the humility that comes from wisdom. But if you harbor *bitter envy* and selfish ambition in your hearts, do not boast about it or deny the truth. Such "wisdom" does not come down from heaven but is earthly, unspiritual, demonic. For where you have *envy* and selfish ambition, there you *find disorder and every evil practice*. (Jas. 3:13–16, emphasis mine)

> Let us behave decently, as in the daytime, not in carousing and drunkenness, not in sexual immorality and debauchery, *not in dissension and jealousy*. (Rom. 13:13)

> I am afraid that when I come I may not find you as I want you to be. . . . I fear that there may be *discord, jealousy, fits of rage, selfish ambition, slander, gossip, arrogance and disorder*. (2 Cor. 12:20, emphasis mine)

> The acts of the flesh are obvious: sexual immorality, impurity and debauchery; idolatry and witchcraft; *hatred, discord, jealousy, fits of rage, selfish ambition, dissensions, factions and envy*; drunkenness, orgies, and the like. I warn you, as I did before, that those who live like this will not inherit the kingdom of God. (Gal. 5:20–21, emphasis mine)

Is it possible to miss the implications of such straightforward biblical teaching? In Romans 13, Paul outlines in great detail the Love-First creed, but then in 13:11–14 he adds the "so what" in light of living in the last days, with the final victory of light over darkness. Paul calls for the abandonment of a carnal course of life and for the Christian to be clothed with Christ. This means that the dissensions rooted in envy are associated not with Christ but with the deeds of darkness. This same theme is carried throughout the New Testament.

Envy is a seed that emerges in dissension, discord, fits of rage, selfish ambition, slander, gossip, arrogance, and every disorder. It should not surprise us that Paul has to caution the church in Corinth about their lack of decency and their abandonment of order (1 Cor. 14:40). Sadly, this passage has become another casualty of *un*conditioned orthodoxy. I've heard this passage quoted to make rules about clapping or not clapping in church, or about whether or not communion trays could be passed from the back or the front.

I'm not including this for sarcasm, but as real examples of our fundamental problem: envy, and not the order of worship, is the root of the lack of decency among Christians and the disorder of their relationships. This is what happens when we do not root our creed in the Love-First command of Christ. Envy is not orthodoxy. Envy is like a superbug, a virus, that keeps mutating until it destroys the host and infects nearly everyone in its circle of influence.

A man came to me and told me he was leaving our church because he just didn't fit in the "BMW crowd." When I asked him to tell me more, he was incensed. "Look out in the parking lot, man! What do you see? BMWs everywhere!"

For just a moment I thought, "Sweet! Someone has taken my '97 Nissan Sentra and left me a brand new Beamer!" But I didn't say it, and I wouldn't have. I could see what was happening to my brother "under the hood." He was struggling with envy. Of course, there were BMWs in the parking lot, right alongside the Sentras, Caravans, and Explorers. But his envy had infected his eyesight and affected his insight.

Over and over Jesus's detractors heard his words, twisted them, and then told their lies like they were truth. Jesus many times remarked, "He who has ears let him hear." And it was envy that motivated them to craft a plan for his demise (Mark 15:10). Their accusations were "true to them" because they believed every thought they had about Jesus. It didn't matter if his words or actions actually matched their accusations. No evidence was necessary. How could such an unjust plan catch fire? Envy.

James answers the rhetorical question, "Why do you Christians fight so much?" The answer is not complicated: envy, jealousy and covetousness have so skewed our motives that we believe our destruction of others is both justified and a sign of our fidelity to the faith (4:1–6). James, Paul, and Jesus disapproved of such unholy rationalizing. In my experience I have found that when envy is running the show, James, Paul, and Jesus are invoked as a supporting cast, not invited to center stage.

But notice that Jesus was the antithesis of his accusers. There was no hint of discord, dissension, fits of rage, or slander. In fact, he fulfilled Isaiah's prophecy.

> He was oppressed and afflicted, *yet he did not open his mouth*; he was led like a lamb to the slaughter, and as a sheep before its shearers is silent, *so he did not open his mouth.* By oppression and judgment he was taken away. Yet who of his generation protested? For he was cut off from the land of the living; for the transgression of my people he was punished. He was assigned a grave with the wicked, and with the rich in his death, *though he had done no violence, nor was any deceit in his mouth.* (Isa. 53:7–9, emphasis mine)

As Peter appeals for transformed relationships in the body of Christ and beyond, he quotes this prophecy and recalls the cross,

> To this you were called, because Christ suffered for you, leaving you an example, that you should follow in his steps. "He committed no sin, and no deceit was found in his mouth." When they hurled their insults at him, he did not retaliate; when he suffered, he made no threats. Instead, he entrusted himself to him who judges justly. (1 Pet. 2:21–23)

Jesus displayed his unequivocal commitment to the conditions of divine love. Those who were blinded by envy now witnessed the full display of envy-less love. Their accusations were met with affection; their fits of rage were confounded by the finished work of divine compassion.

> Jealousy (envy) is one of the deadly sins. Nothing can more thoroughly embitter the human spirit and poison personal relationships than a spirit of envy or jealousy. It was the direct cause of the first crime in the story of the human race (Genesis 4:1–8). Envy is the scarlet thread of unholy passion that runs not only through the church in Corinth but through all human life.[1]

Envy is more than just the struggle to make emotional and psychological peace with the inequities of natural giftedness or blessing.

> Envy is a sin, and a sin is like an infected wound: the infection spreads. Envy is an infected wound in the soul and it breeds further infection: it begets hatred, hatred begets strife. Only Christian love is pure and strong enough to endure differences in status and circumstance that are inevitable, just as Christian love alone is strong enough and pure enough to endow with graciousness those who are so blessed. Paul saw the spirit of love as the only hope for unity in the disordered Corinthian church.[2]

The Corinthians were disconnected from the conditions of Christ's love. The results were internally and externally destructive. Paul didn't attempt to "make nice" with the different factions and figure out a way to compromise them all back into the pews for Sunday worship. This would have been nothing but an empty show, contemptible to God, corruptible to the body of Christ, and costly to the waiting and watching world. No, Paul called this church he loved back to obedience to the Christ-creed, the orthodoxy of divine love. Unconditioned love had put them in this ditch, and only Christ-conditioned love would get them out.

Love-First Reflections

- From 1 Corinthians 13:4–6, write down the two "Love is" statements and the eight "Love is not" statements.

Love is . . .	Love is not . . .

- Which doctrine does the church drift away from on "its path toward division"?

- Why do you think jealousy and envy are potentially so deadly?

- Using an Internet search engine like Google, or using a Bible concordance, look up biblical characters who suffered from the ailment of jealousy and make a note of each reference.

- What is our only hope for healing?

11

LOVE IS NOT BOASTFUL OR PROUD

Healthy love is not boastful or proud. These two conditions—boasting and pride—must be studied together, although their distinctiveness is contributing to the problems in Corinth. These two words may almost seem extraneous in this list, perhaps the least problems of the eight in Paul's list. We are so used to political blowhards and athletes "talkin' smack" that boasting is an accepted form of expression in nearly every layer of our society. It may be helpful to note, however, that how people boast varies from culture to culture. People in Hong Kong, China, and Asia, for instance, will not boast in the same way that people in New York, the United States, and traditionally European cultures boast. But we all do boast.

Why does this behavior have so much traction? To begin with, because boasting is related to envy. Envy is our response when we feel like someone else has something that we don't. This can lead to judgments of inferiority on both ends: You feel inferior because you "don't seem to measure up," but you consider the others inferior because "they don't deserve the attention, respect, or reward they are enjoying." This is where boasting and pride sneak in and wreck love.

Boasting is a way of differentiating ourselves from others, thus concluding that our differences make us superior. The reason this does not qualify as love is because the love Paul is advocating is not human benevolence, which can actually lead to pride (Matt. 6:5–8). Instead, Christian love is the tangible provision of kindness and patience to the undeserved, the marginalized, the hidden, the person who cannot pay us back in kind, or to our enemy. To be sure, the word *love* in English has many lower associations, but the Christ-conditioned love Paul seeks to form in the Corinthians and in us is of the highest calling.

Boasting is the external display of pride, an internal disposition. Both are equally destructive. Boasting cannot survive without pride, and pride is rarely satisfied—not for long, at least—without boasting.

The boasting to which Paul refers thrives in rhetoric. It is the creating of ideas, emotions, and reactions that do not require reality. In Paul's correspondence with the Corinthian church, boasting and pride are consistent themes. They value sounding impressive and receiving accolades more than fact, function, or benefit.

The divisions in that church are fanned into flame by their boasting. So in the first chapter of his first letter Paul writes, "I appeal to you, brothers and sisters, in the name of our Lord Jesus Christ, that all of you agree with one another in what you say and that *there be no divisions among you*, but that you be perfectly united in mind and thought." He tells them that some of Chloe's clan have informed him that "*there are quarrels among you*." God is not impressed by the showy, pretentious things that impress some folks, Paul reminds them. All we Christians really have to boast about is Christ, so, as the Scriptures command, "Let the one who boasts boast in the Lord." To make his point, he reminds them of the example he set for them (1 Cor. 2:1–5).

Later in the letter, we find the boasting hidden in subtle forms of veiled superiority. People in Corinth love their giftedness because it is a way to get attention—and not the good kind. They like finding their way to the stage to be "super spiritual." Their vocal gifts make them bigger than life. Their eloquence is like a personal billboard of self-importance.

When we read chapters 11–14 in this letter, we see relational rifts between rich and poor, male and female, and people with different gifts. What has been interpreted as a discussion of gender in chapters 11 and 14 is actually about self-promotion. Many understand these chapters as restricting women from praying or prophesying in the public assembly (the supposed questions of orthodoxy). The contextual problem Paul is addressing actually is their lack of Christ-conditioned love, specifically the divine love that precludes boasting.

Paul's language is not difficult to grasp. When we do not commune in love, it is not communion. If we exercise spiritual gifts without love, they are not spiritual. When we hold one leader in our church in higher esteem than another because they champion our creeds and causes, we are not obedient to the law of Christ, nor are we in line with the truth of the gospel. When we boast about the grace we show to some while callously running down others, we are neither holy nor loving. These are hard truths from Paul's pen, but he knows the Love-First Christ-creed. He knows that all—yes, *all*—of these things are worthless without love.

In 1 Corinthians 8–10, Paul deals with a first-century hot potato: what do we do with brothers and sisters who are in Christ but who still have some beliefs and practices from their history in idolatry? How would we approach their questions?

- Is there one God or many?

- Can we still go to those temples?
- If we buy meat that was offered to false gods, are we (by proxy) participating in idolatry?
- If I am invited to dinner by someone who still worships idols, is it okay for me to go and hang out with them? What do I do if someone sees me there?

How would you take on this list of questions if you were Paul? He knows their struggles, and the stakes are great. But his response is insightful. "Now about food sacrificed to idols," he begins. "We know that 'We all possess knowledge.' But *knowledge puffs up while love builds up*. Those who think they know something do not yet know as they ought to know. But whoever loves God is known by God" (8:1–3, emphasis mine).

When knowledge is valued above love, it *puffs us up*. This is the same word used in 1 Corinthians 13:4 for "boastful." Love-conditioned knowledge understands what to do with what we know. In this passage, "knowledge" and knowing God are not the same thing. Paul echoes John's instruction: "Dear friends, let us love one another, for love comes from God. Everyone who loves has been born of God and knows God. *Whoever does not love does not know God*, because God is love" (1 John 4:7–8, emphasis mine).

Some might point out that Paul can emphasize love because they have all the knowledge they need. Notice, however, the NIV translators' choice to put the statement about possessing knowledge in quotes. This suggests that, as in several other comments in 1 Corinthians, Paul is quoting their mantra, not his. This translation decision is backed up by 8:7a, 10–11:

> But *not everyone* possesses this knowledge. For if someone with a weak conscience sees you, with all *your knowledge*, eating in an idol's temple, won't that person be emboldened to eat what is sacrificed to idols? So

> this weak brother or sister, for whom Christ died, is *destroyed by your knowledge.*

Here is the issue: knowing the Bible "backward and forward" counts for nothing if we do not love according to the Christ-conditions. Not only must we love, but we must embrace the conditions Christ lays down for divinely inspired love.

The pain of 1 Corinthians morphs into a full-scale emotional storm by the time Paul writes 2 Corinthians. Some in Corinth are questioning Paul's credentials, asserting that he is not even a true apostle. His heart is broken, but not his commitment to the conditions of love. Paul remains faithful to them, willing to be humiliated in their eyes to help them see that they have fallen into the very thing he has warned against: empty boasts. Twice as many references to boasting appear in Paul's letters to the Corinthians as in the rest of the New Testament books combined. Their church is a mess. If you really want to mess up a church, give up on Christ-conditioned love and let pride take over. Here are some snippets from Paul's second letter:

> As surely as the truth of Christ is in me, nobody in the regions of Achaia will stop this boasting of mine. Why? Because I do not love you? God knows I do! And I will keep on doing what I am doing in order to cut the ground from under those who want an opportunity to be considered equal with us in the things they boast about. For such people are false apostles, deceitful workers, masquerading as apostles of Christ. (11:10–13)

Paul is on fire. This church is in shambles because some people are trying to elevate themselves above others. Their boasting is a devilish way to shove Paul out and put themselves in as the leaders.

I know this scenario can be hard to imagine, but it is common. A friend of mine, fresh out of seminary at his first ministry appointment, discovered that another minister was embezzling money from their church's offerings. This newly minted minister was young, inexperienced, and frightened. Quickly he confronted the pilfering pastor, who then explained that the young minister misunderstood what he was doing and that he should be ashamed for questioning him. To make matters worse, this young preacher was then warned by a former minister of that church not to tarnish his own reputation by getting another minister fired, so the thefts continued.

My young friend then received a call from the board president of a Christian camp, who reported some "suspicious concerns" about the way the older pastor had handled the camp finances. The board representative's call was another red flag on a growing heap of red flags. Finally, the treasurer from a local senior citizen ministry called for a meeting with the young minister to report that he had caught this same pastor pilfering funds from them. Three strikes, right? Wrong!

The older pastor had cleverly created a story about himself over the years, extolling his integrity and trustworthiness so that if someone ever questioned his handling of money, he would strongly reiterate his "untainted" record. His boasting had worked. He continued stealing for months, while the church leaders expressed their great disappointment in the young minister's suspicion toward his older colleague.

Eventually a university development officer from another state called to ask how this same older pastor was "handling his cancer treatments." He had received a letter from the older pastor asking for financial help with his mounting medical bills. My friend reported that the older pastor didn't have cancer, and that he must be thinking of someone else. The fund-raiser was shaken. By the time the story broke, the thieving minister had already received over eight thousand dollars in donations! The local church leaders finally called him to account and fired him.

My friend reflected often on the powerful delusion these church leaders were under because of the dishonest pastor's empty boasting that had gone on for decades. The Corinthians could have warned this young pastor and his church of the clear signs of impending disaster because they went through it themselves. When boasting gains momentum, it creates an alternative reality based on alternative facts, and truth is sacrificed. Instead of getting drawn into this distraction from his commitment to love first, Paul chooses to model a different approach. Where he could boast (which he knows is completely useless and fruitless), he shares a personal story about being caught up into heaven to share a shoulder-to-shoulder moment with God. Paul knows this vision is a spiritual trump card, a there's-no-way-to-top-this story, but instead of leveraging it for personal gain, Paul turns the story into an anti-boasting lesson.

> But I will not boast about myself, except about my weaknesses. . . . *Therefore, in order to keep me from becoming conceited, I was given a thorn in my flesh,* a messenger of Satan, to torment me. Three times I pleaded with the Lord to take it away from me. But he said to me, "My grace is sufficient for you, for my power is made perfect in weakness." *Therefore I will boast all the more gladly about my weaknesses,* so that Christ's power may rest on me. (2 Cor. 12:5b, 7b–9, emphasis mine)

Addicted to self-promotion and self-gratification, the boastful Corinthian leaders were cannibalizing their fans. They were destroying their church.

In our culture boasting must be subtle, or it is received negatively. There are four primary categories of what I term, "bearable boasting" that we actually allow:

- When others are boasting about a win that we approve.

- When others demean a person, team, candidate, or group of whom we disapprove.
- A form of boasting called "credentialing" (building self up in order to make people believe your opinion is important, versus simply stating the opinion and letting it stand or fall based on its own merit).
- Boasting as a social bully. This includes making claims with such force that others will think twice before they question anything you say.

You may wonder why I dubbed this "bearable boasting." Consider Paul's words, "In fact, you even put up with anyone who enslaves you or exploits you or takes advantage of you or puts on airs or slaps you in the face" (2 Cor. 11:20).

Bearable boasting is most effective in religious environments where pretension is wrapped in false spiritual motives. Christians often cloak their arrogance in the name of "correcting error" or "marking a false brother." Under such pretense, anything goes. There is no humility to this. This is simply the outcome of a life unconditioned by Christ's Love-First creed.

The opposite of boastful pride is complete humility. Jesus holds up the "poor in spirit" as the first of his *be*-attitudes. The humble are receptive to Jesus's conditions, getting rid of all malice and slander, then being clothed with Christ in love. The Corinthians wanted to be seen and heard; the humble want to serve and share. For the prideful, no honor is too great; for the humble, no opportunity to serve is too low. The attitude of Jesus is held up for imitation, but notice the word, *attitude*. Humility is a *mindset*. As the apostle Paul calls on the Corinthians to embody the mind of Christ, this humility is defined by Christ himself. If the Roman church had left their mail open on the counter, we would read this note from Paul: "Let love be genuine; hate what is evil, hold fast to what is good; love one another with mutual affection; outdo one another in showing honor (Rom. 12:9–10, NRSV)."

But how do we get from point A to point B? How do we genuinely move from prideful boasting to preferring one another in honor? The fact that we are humans does not make this easy! We determine to be humble and the next thing we know someone else is boasting. We fear seeming unimportant or getting left behind. We envy the elevation of the other person and we at least have to keep pace. If we really don't like that person all that much, we feel the necessity to cut them down to size in the eyes of others.

My dad would have a word for us: "Who you respect says more about you than it does about them." I bring him up because he grew to where he was at peace with others receiving the honor and attention. Perhaps that makes some sense of his favorite Bible verse, which is inscribed on his grave marker:

> Therefore, I urge you, brothers and sisters, in view of God's mercy, to offer your bodies as a living sacrifice, holy and pleasing to God—this is your true and proper worship. Do not conform to the pattern of this world, but be transformed by the renewing of your mind. Then you will be able to test and approve what God's will is—his good, pleasing and perfect will. (Rom. 12:1–2)

And this lays the foundation for humility-conditioned love described by Paul in the next verse: "Through the grace given to me I say to everyone among you not to think more highly of himself than he ought to think." Humility-conditioned love is the antidote to the poison of boasting pride. Humility is attractive and compelling.

The community outreach of our church is felt in thousands of surprisingly subtle ways. Every week hundreds of our neighbors come to our campus for recovery meetings ranging from sexual challenges, drug and alcohol addictions, and eating disorders. Spouses and children reeling from the upheaval of divorce find a caring and dynamic community. People suffering through loss find help, empathy, and a path forward through Grief Share. Then there are hundreds of families who participate in our preschool, after-school programs, and sports leagues. Our counseling center, diverse and bilingual, provides hope and healing for both our church and our community.

Why do I share this? Does it sound like boasting? I am actually sharing this with you because all of these ministries thrive *without* boasting. There are no billboards, no write-ups in the paper, no shout-outs from the rooftop. There are just thousands of hugs, smiles, prayers, and hours devoted to one message: You are loved, welcomed, honored. And people feel it.

Love-First Reflections

- Read the following statements. Circle the one that best describes your experience with pride and boasting.

  Boasting cannot survive without pride.
  Pride is rarely satisfied without boasting.
  Boasting is an external display of pride.
  Pride is an internal disposition of boasting.

- Fill in the blanks. (Hint: they are all the same word!)

  If we do not commune in ________, we are not actually in communion.
  Spiritual gifts without ________, are unspiritual.
  All things, without ________, are worthless.
  Knowledge puffs up, while ________ builds up.
  Knowledge makes us feel important, but it is ________ that strengthens the church.

- Read and meditate on Philippians 2:3–11. Journal your thoughts on how we can move from the selfishness of trying to impress others to humbly valuing others above ourselves.

- Why do you think Jesus taught that the humble "will inherit the whole earth" (Matt. 5:5 NLT)?)

LOVE IS NOT RUDE

Rudeness is cultural. Rudeness is relational. What is considered rude in one culture or relationship may not have the same effect in another.

On my first trip to Kazakhstan in 2002, the older Almaty airport terminal was in the process of being replaced with a sparkling new facility that opened two years later. My departure gate was in the older section that looked like familiar former Soviet Union architecture. It was sparse on aesthetics, but it would withstand a nuclear blast. The doors were narrow, and the seating area cramped. I arrived several hours early for my flight and positioned myself near the door to the jet bridge. Early bird catches the worm, right?

When the gate area had filled and the call was made to board the flight, a sudden rush of humanity broke loose. "These people know nothing of lines," I thought. "What is the matter with them?" Suddenly, I was trapped in the crush of the crowd as the mob shuffled toward the door like a herd of sheep through a narrow shoot. I was appalled, incensed, and feeling very Western—superior and

Western. These folks simply had not advanced far enough yet to know how important it is to the social order, safety, and advancement of humanity to stand in lines. How rude!

I arrived at my seat, now bound to fly for several hours with these non-liner-uppers. What else do they not know how to do correctly? But then, because we were boarded, seated, and ready to depart thirty minutes in advance of taxi and takeoff, I had time to reflect.

- Room for my overhead bag
- Comfortable seat
- Thirty minutes early
- Normal amount of time for boarding
- No one was upset *but me*

Sooooooo . . . these people are happy, excited to fly, comfortable and laughing. I am miffed, pouting, self-seeking, and counting their wrongs against them (wait . . . I'm getting ahead of myself here!). I had judged *them*, but *I* was the rude dude on that plane.

Rudeness had become a part of the Corinthian church culture. Imagine them like a thermostat: they adjusted everything to match *their* comfort and preferences. Multiple commentaries on 1 Corinthians note that the negative qualities of rudeness, self-seeking, easily angered, and keeping a record of wrongs unite to form a coherent profile of the trouble at Corinth. They had normalized these socially destructive qualities, and now their relationships are showing the strain of such negative turmoil.

"Rudeness" is a softer word than what we see in the original language of Scripture. The first-century thought conveys something more akin to *shameful*, *indecent*, *ugly behavior*, *to dishonor another*. The idea is not just cutting in line or forgetting to hold the door. It means more like, "I do not care how my behavior negatively impacts your life on a micro or macro level." In the Kazakhstan airport, my Western idea that getting there early meant I should get on the airplane before anyone else suggests that my values, centered on me, demean or negate other's values.

So in the case of the crowding Kazaks, my actions demonstrated that I didn't really care about their social values. I didn't care to learn their custom of honoring community over individuality, honoring older people ahead of younger. How could I have represented myself, my faith, and even my country better? What if my social interaction had been first conditioned by love, love that is not rude?

Rudeness isn't a fixed behavior worldwide, or even from family to family, *but it is an attitude*. Rudeness suggests that I care more about how you respond to me than how I represent Christ-conditioned love. Rudeness is a symptom of an *un*conditioned life, and we will have to care more about God's love than about our own personal likes if this is going to change.

Many people choose rude behavior to "teach others a lesson." It is a look, a tone of voice, or a comment that indicates superiority and inferiority. My disgruntled body language on the airplane in Almaty was a signal to the line-crashers that I did not like their behavior and that I thought they should change. I valued my own way of thinking so much that I cut myself free from the conditions of love. Their behavior displeased me enough that I was now validated in treating them rudely.

I have also come across people who believe that their rude behavior is a sign of their integrity. They disapprove of another person so much that being patient and kind would be unacceptable. It would be fake and they would therefore not be acting with integrity. So their rude and demeaning behavior is their way of expressing their integrity. With some folks I know, this has gone on for years. My guess is that somewhere along the line, the whole "not keeping a record of wrongs" also went out the window, along with Jesus's annoying "splinter and beam" teaching. But this is the trap of rudeness. I imagine that I am superior, so I am. In the airplane in Almaty, they didn't care. They enjoyed themselves while I fumed. I felt pretty stupid.

This word for rudeness is used throughout 1 Corinthians to describe the unloving behavior of the Corinthian Christians toward one another. Perhaps the most poignant example is their self-satisfying "Communion" service. This is the ultimate oxymoron—a self-gratifying time of Communion. It is so ridiculous that Paul tells them that even though they are breaking the bread and drinking the wine of Eucharist, it is *not* the Lord's Supper they are taking. What does this mean? In the light of 1 Corinthians 13:1–3, it means that even if we go through the actions of the Lord's Supper, if our attitude toward others is one of unconditioned rudeness, then we are nails on a chalkboard. We have done nothing and are nothing.

This idea is not new with Paul. The prophet Isaiah pours out an extended indictment of *un*conditioned religious action, along with an invitation to authenticity. After scolding his people for their public display of show-off humility in their worship and fasting, he told them what God really wanted from them:

> Is not this the kind of fasting I have chosen: to loose the chains of injustice and untie the cords of the yoke, to set the oppressed free and break every yoke? Is it not to share your food with the hungry and to provide the poor wanderer with shelter—when you see the naked, to clothe them, and not to turn away from your own flesh and blood? . . . Then you will call, and the Lord will answer; you will cry for help, and he will say: Here am I. (58:6–9a)

To restore their relationship with the Lord, Isaiah told his people they had to stop their rudeness toward one another. He echoed Paul's description of authentic love: "If you do away with the yoke of oppression, with the pointing finger and malicious talk, and if you spend yourselves in behalf of the hungry and satisfy the needs of the oppressed, then your light will rise in the darkness . . ." (58:9b–10). Every time I read this text in Isaiah I am convicted and encouraged. It honestly feels like my life, my church, and my world. I want so badly to be a Repairer of Broken Walls. And, as research reveals, so do most of us.

Robert Putnam and David Campbell in their book *American Grace: How Religion Divides and Unites Us* write that "regular churchgoers are more than twice as likely to volunteer to help the needy, compared to demographically matched Americans who rarely if ever attend church."[1] In response to this observation, Douglas Jacobsen comments, "A quick look beneath the surface rhetoric of American religion reveals that most American Christians are not pugnacious culture warriors. Instead they are religious do-gooders in the best sense of that term, people who are ready to come to the aid of anyone needing help."[2]

So, if we Christians are soft-hearted, charitable souls, how do we explain our deplorable reputation for rudeness?

If you google "Why are Christians rude?" you will meet blogging preachers and angry atheists, and the thread is pretty straightforward: Christians *can* be nice, but they are appallingly mean. Although I cannot repeat some of the language used online to describe Christian rudeness (that's oxymoronic, right?), here is a helpful sampling of answers to our question, "Why are Christians rude?"

> "Because they think that just because they walk in a building to believe in their god that they're better than us average people."

> "Cause most of them think there [sic] better than anyone. This is a good part reason why I just stop going to church. If God accepts people like that idk [I don't know] if I wanna go then."

> "I say we burn the bibles, close the churches . . . it creates prejudice among the fellow man . . . wars almost always involve religion."

From there, it only went downhill . . . until I read a response under the online identity, **Psalm 14–1**, who posted, "I can't speak for other Christians . . . but I am not better than ANYBODY. The Apostle Paul calls himself the chief sinner in 1 Tim. 1:15, but believe me, I am the lowest of the low . . . God's grace is the reason that you and I are no better than each other . . . I pray that helps some." To which a responder under the online identity, **Thanks,** replied, "Your words inspired me today. Thank you for posting!! I'm new to the area and looking for a church. I'm hoping to find a place that won't look down on me. People can be nasty, but I guess that's on them. Thank you again."[3]

Perhaps the person posting under the online identity **Psalm 14–1** isn't verifiably the lowest of the low, but this post captured the real issue. Rudeness wounds. This post revealed personal hurt. And **Psalm 14–1** grasped what was at stake.

In his first letter to the Corinthians, Paul encourages them to go ahead and rather be wronged than to bash each other in the public courts (6:7). He tells them he will personally go vegetarian if that's the language love speaks to some of his struggling brothers and sisters (8:9–13). He delivers what is to me his most emotion-packed appeal in 9:12, 21–22 when he writes,

> On the contrary, *we put up with anything* rather than hinder the gospel of Christ. . . . To those not having the law I became like one not having the law (though I am not free from God's law *but am under Christ's law*), so as to win those not having the law. To the weak I became weak, to win the weak. *I have become all things to all people* so that by all possible means I might save some. [Emphasis mine.]

Tom, another responder, epitomizes the false dichotomy of "holding to the truth," while abandoning the Love-First creed and his conditioned love:

> When it comes to nonbelievers, showing them manners is a way of saying, "please hang around." [But] I don't want some Satanist influencing my kids, family or community! I'd rather be blunt and considered "rude" than idly sit by and allow these faith-bashing pagans to destroy everything good and decent in my life. I encourage all true Christians to do whatever it takes to expel all the agents of Satan from our community who will not accept the Truth of Jesus Christ."

Tom is concerned with "truth" but disconnected from divine love. What is "accepting the truth of Jesus" if it is not faithfully obeying the conditions of his first and greatest commands? Is **Tom**'s Bible missing the scriptures we've studied in this book? Or is **Tom**, like many of us, religiously conditioned to live an *un*conditioned orthodoxy that leaves out the Love-First creed?

Living the Christ-conditioned life means that I love without being rude. So for **Tom** and me, Jesus is unyielding on this point; love is not rude, whether it is in the Kazakhstan airport or in your own backyard.

Love-First Reflections

- True_____ or False_____ The perception of "what is rude" can vary from culture to culture. What significance should this have on how you interact with people of other cultures you meet in your travels or in your daily life?

- What happens to your inner spiritual health, and the health of your relationships with others when you value your own way of thinking as *superior* over everyone else?

- Read Isaiah 58:9–10; Philippians 2:14–15; Matthew 5:14–16. What similar themes do you discover overlapping in these three texts? How do they challenge the way you think about rudeness versus Love-First in your relationships?

- Fill in the blank: "We ______ ______ with anything rather than ______________ the ______________ of Christ." (1 Corinthians 9:12b) What role does Love-First play in honoring the gospel of Christ? What are some steps you can take to better follow Paul's strong example in this verse?

LOVE IS NOT SELF-SEEKING

"There is someone I love, even though I don't approve of what he does. There is someone I accept, though some of his thoughts and actions revolt me. There is someone I forgive, though he hurts the people I love the most. That person is me."[1]

—Adapted from C. S. Lewis

I was driving with an older gentleman in my car. I knew from others that he was living a powerful story of marital forgiveness. Now was my chance to hear for myself, but how open would he be to sharing? I didn't want to be intrusive, but I also didn't want to miss the wisdom and insight for which he was respected among the brothers in our church. My reticence and his humility were no match for the nudging of the Spirit. So I gingerly asked, "What are some things you wish every husband knew?" He replied, "Well, you can't really know if you love someone until they give you a reason not to."

"Are you serious?" I thought. "Do I want to ask anything else?" But before I could ask him my next question, he shared more. "Let me tell you what I mean," he expanded. "I knew before my wife's affair became public that she was struggling. I didn't know she was having an affair, but I knew she was coming undone. When it all came out, I didn't know where to go. The man in the affair had been a friend. As painful as the betrayal was, I don't really hold anything against either of them any longer." Then he touched my soul by saying matter-of-factly, "*Things happen in life, and sometimes they happen to you.*" He continued, "I knew I had to try to build a bridge to her, and even to him. It took some time, a lot of time, because neither of them felt worthy of a bridge."

Things happen in life, and sometimes they happen to you.

My mind was racing. His honest, loving words produced so many questions. I hadn't met very many people who gave such careful, yet spiritual thought to such bitter circumstances. "Did you ever think of divorcing her?" I asked.

"Sure," he replied. "I thought about it. It wasn't easy, and I don't think everyone should do exactly what I did, but I had to be honest with myself. I still wanted to be married to her. I couldn't make her want me, but had I divorced her, it would have been for everyone else but me. My family and friends put a lot of pressure on me to divorce her, but I knew that was not what I wanted, so I didn't."

My mind was paralyzed. It's hard to explain, but his situation and the way he was describing it were otherworldly, like something from heaven and not from earth. He thought about his life in ways I had never seriously considered. Read his words over again and contemplate what they meant to him, and what they might mean to whatever you are going through.

He didn't feel targeted by God for the troubles he and his wife faced. He recognized that these kinds of heartaches are happening around us throughout life, but we don't give them our full attention until they happen to us. But he also didn't use the depth of his pain as an excuse to depart from his faith. He continued, "I took a vow, and I aimed to keep my vow. Besides, she needed to know she was worth more than the mistakes she made, and I was in a unique position to show her that."

I have officiated at hundreds of weddings. Most of them have been a real joy. Every single one of them included an exchange of vows. Sometimes people chose the traditional vows, others wrote their own, and sometimes they requested that I write custom vows for them. In every single wedding the vows were directional—they pointed people toward a life where each would be the absolute best they could be so that the marriage would be a blessing to both. You know the vows. Hopefully they are a way for each partner to say that, "whatever happens on your end, I aim to be the person these vows represent."

Look at this gentleman's statement again: "I took a vow, and I aimed to keep my vow."

Nowhere in his reply was there anything about *her* vow. Just his. She gave him reasons to not keep his vow, but he saw his vow as both a responsibility and an opportunity. He could seek her best good. And he could seek her best good whether she reconciled or not. Whatever action he took would be conditioned by a love that was not self-seeking.

Christ-conditioned love lives to give. Unconditioned love seeks to get. When Paul writes that love is not self-seeking, he means that love does not pour its energies into relational transactions that ultimately benefit self. Jesus tells us to "seek first his kingdom and his righteousness" and everything else we need will be provided (Matt. 6:33). This is not hard to understand, but it is difficult to live. When we seek first the Kingdom of God we see others in a different light. They are no longer commodities for our consumption, assets to satisfy our appetites, or competitors to be conquered.

Both James and Paul affirm this condition set by Jesus. James writes, "If you harbor bitter envy and *selfish ambition* in your hearts, do not boast about it or deny the truth" (3:14). And Paul echoes the instruction: "*Do nothing out of selfish ambition* or vain conceit. Rather, in humility value others above yourselves, not looking to your own interests but each of you to the interests of the others" (Phil. 2:3–4).

I've often heard people quip that they would love to be able to sit down with Jesus "because they've got a lotta questions." But when we read the Gospels, we can see that asking Jesus questions can really blow up a person's life. Remember the lawyer we looked at in Luke 10, the fellow who set up Jesus to share the story of the Good Samaritan by asking Jesus a question? "Teacher," he asked, "what must I do to inherit eternal life?" Out of respect for his inquisitor's profession, Jesus answered the question with two of his own, and both were intentional. He asked him first, "What is written in the Law?" Then he pressed him, "How do you read it?"

I am not sure if the lawyer was nervous leading into the conversation with the miracle-working Rabbi, but he had to feel great when Jesus hit him in the sweet spot! You probably recall that he answered with the Old Testament laws that command, "Love the Lord your God," and, "Love your neighbor." As we discussed earlier, Jesus gave this man's answer the orthodox stamp of approval. "You have answered correctly (*orthos*)," Jesus replied. "Do this and you will live."

As we look at this memorable event again, this time I want to consider Jesus's second question: "How do you read it?" The word translated by this phrase was used as an emphatic statement of reading or perceiving something accurately. This was the word often used to describe the reading of Scripture publicly. Later this word also came to mean "to recognize." Jesus was asking this man to make a stab at exegesis by emphasis. Let me explain what I mean.

When I was in undergrad, I took a class titled, "Oral Interpretation of Scripture." The class was challenging, eye-opening, and life-changing. It was taught by a legendary speech professor who was also dean of the Communications Department of our university. He was extremely exacting. In the class each student was assigned a passage of scripture. Outside of class the student would then research the original languages, commentaries, and history of interpretation. The student would then write a paper detailing what was believed to be the correct interpretation of the text.

But here's the kicker. When we came to class, the student was allowed to read or quote only the *exact* text—not one word more or one word less. All of the work of exegesis and interpretation had to be expressed through vocal inflection, rhythm, tone, and emphasis. This exercise was repeated three times during the semester. It proved to be invaluable. I learned that the emphasis I placed on one word or even one syllable, coupled with the speed I chose for one phrase over another, could make all the difference in how the meaning and impact of the passage were understood by the hearers.

When Jesus asked this expert in Scripture, "What does the Law of Moses say, and how do you read it?" he was listening for more than a recitation of words. He listened to find out how this man "read and perceived it," how he would *apply* to life what he was reading. When the man delivered his initial response, Jesus affirmed his genuine orthodoxy. The passages he quoted and the meaning he gave to them are the key to life. But the man revealed something that proves to be the undoing of many. Rather than seeking and submitting to the conditions of these dual love commands, he followed the *un*conditioned life of the self-seeking. He didn't want to be held accountable to the implications of the doctrine.

The Law expert asked Jesus a question that might go over the head of the average Western Christian, "Who is my neighbor?" Two important background notes add texture to the picture Luke paints for us.

First, Jewish rabbinical teaching from the second century BC included the following teaching:

> When you do a good deed, make sure you know who is benefiting from it; then what you do will not be wasted. You will be repaid for any kindness you show to a devout person. If he doesn't repay you, the Most High will. No good ever comes to a person who gives comfort to the wicked; it is not a righteous act. *Give to religious people, but don't help sinners. . . . The Most High himself hates sinners,* and he will punish them. *Give to good people, but do not help sinners.* (Sirach 12:1–4, 6, emphasis mine)

If you're familiar with the Gospels, you know the Samaritans were *not* on the "good" people list for this lawyer nor for the Pharisees (John 4:9). But for an expert in the Law, Torah certainly carried more weight than the Wisdom of Sirach. Where was this man to turn to find a way out of the social benevolence required by divine love?

Second, the Pharisees, along with another influential group, the Sadducees, dominated Jewish religious life during the ministry of Jesus. The Pharisees were known for a literal interpretation of Torah, while they accused the Sadducees of a more "liberal" interpretation. Part of the *un*orthodox teaching of the Pharisees was that in some way every Jew was to fulfill a priestly role. This meant that holiness and pure living should go beyond the walls of the temple and into every aspect of life. This expert in the Law knew that his orthodox answer to Jesus implied a priestly responsibility to the people he met along the way . . . that is, unless he could find a loophole.

Rather than a direct answer which could turn into a debate (no offense to my attorney friends, but this guy was a lawyer, after all!), Jesus told him, and us, a story. But this is no ordinary story. No storyteller before Jesus or after has risen to his caliber. He weaves the earthly and otherworldly together in such seamless fashion that the listener cannot feel the transition until it has already encompassed him. You may have heard the story of the Good Samaritan your entire life, so it may surprise you to learn who the main character of the story is. who the main character is. I would suggest . . . the man in the ditch. He is the only character in the story who appears in every verse of the story in Luke 10:30–35.

We call this the story of the Good Samaritan, but he is only "good" because someone needed him to be good. John Nolland, author of the Luke commentary in the *Word Biblical Commentary* series writes, "It is *from the perspective of the ditch* where one lies helpless and battered, and in desperate need of help, that one should reflect upon the question 'who is my neighbor?' Then one will know how wide the reach of neighbor love should extend" (emphasis mine).[2]

Further Nolland notes, "The lawyer wanted an un-principled [*un*conditioned] answer to the scope of neighbor responsibility. Instead, he is invited by the story to look at the neighbor question from the point of view of the potential recipient of neighbor-love in a situation of extremity, for whom the answer to the question can be a matter of life and death."[3] The Samaritan, who would have been declared an enemy on the basis of ethnicity and religion, became a neighbor through compassion.

Nolland continues, "Jesus suggests that we should answer the lawyer's question from the vantage point of isolation and desperate need, and then make use of the same answer when we come to the question from a position of strength"[4]—in other words, when we are in the position to help, will the purpose of neighborly love still be as clear to us as when we were in the ditch?

From the vantage point of the man in the ditch, hopes were raised, and then dashed. The priest was his brightest hope, and the lawyer had to hope the priest would come through. When the priest shunned the needy, it must have thrown the lawyer into frustration and shame. Surely this story would affirm his self-perceived righteousness (and this is a common theme in Luke: 7:29–30; 16:15; 18:9, 21). When the character most closely aligned with the lawyer failed his priestly duty, the story could only go south from there!

The Levite, perhaps another manifestation of the professional priestly caste in the eyes of the lawyer, wasn't really that big of a letdown, though to the man in the ditch that's certainly another story.

When the Samaritan rides onto the scene on a donkey, everything is set right for the man in the ditch and wrong for the poor lawyer. Each added layer of compassion paints the Samaritan, who should be fundamentally flawed, instead as sickeningly kind. The lawyer, whom Jesus placed first in the ditch with the battered man, is now more aware than ever of the life-and-death tangibility of the Love-First creed. There is no way to make a good neighbor out of the priest or the Levite. Their titles and doctrines do not make up for their lack of orthodox love. The self-seeking life of a priest or Levite, *un*conditioned by divine love, is hauntingly dark when exposed by the light of the other-serving, love-conditioned Samaritan.

When Jesus asked the lawyer, "Which of these three do you think was the neighbor to the man who fell into the hands of robbers?" the only satisfactory answer came from the ditch of desperation, "The one who had mercy on him." The lawyer was honest, or the story made him so. I respect him for dropping all charges against Samaritans. His case had been overturned. From the viewpoint of the beaten and battered, only the lovers of others make the grade. With this image now ingrained in his question-asker's soul, Jesus told him, "Go and do likewise."

The Corinthian church was a den of robbers, beating and battering other believers. Casualties were everywhere, but those with influence, status, and position were oblivious to the brothers and sisters they were destroying (1 Cor. 8:11). So Paul drew their attention to the *other-blessing* poverty chosen by Christ (2 Cor. 8:9). and the weakness, fear, and trembling of Paul that were *hard on him but good for them* (1 Cor. 2:3). And Paul also reminded them about God's divine reversal of weak over strong, foolish over wise, and "the things that are not" over "the things that are" that led to their salvation in the first place (1 Cor. 1:20–31).

The message to the Corinthian church is clear: You were in the ditch, desperate and dying. Had you, in your unconditioned, self-seeking ways, happened upon yourself in your sad condition, you, like the priest and Levite, would have walked on by. Yes, you would have left your own sorry self to die in the ditch. But those you hold in low esteem—the patient and kind, the other-serving disciples who have been love-conditioned by Christ—they are the very ones who have loved you so selflessly. So who is the neighbor you can trust to help you—the unconditioned you, or the Christ-conditioned person he is calling you to become?

Self-seeking, or other-serving? One is love and the other is not.

Love-First Reflections

- Read Luke 10:25–37. In verse 26, when Jesus asked the lawyer, "How do you read the Law?" what was Jesus trying to get this man to see about the connection between Love-First and eternal life?

- Would second-century B.C. Jewish rabbis have interpreted the law the same way Jesus did if asked the question, "Who is my neighbor?" Summarize in your own words the quote by Sirach.

- Which perspective does John Nolland call us to take in his commentary on Luke?

- How does the perspective from the ditch help the lawyer to accept Jesus's teachings on what it means to love his neighbor?

- What might the perspective from the ditch look like if Jesus updated the story to the 21st century?

- Who might be the priest, Levite, and Samaritan in today's culture?

- Who is someone you would least likely imagine would be a good neighbor? Why do you judge them that way, and how does this story challenge you?

- Who is someone in the world that might think of *you* as the least likely person who would be a good neighbor to them?

- Take some long moments of self-reflection and write a prayer of personal longing to love like the good neighbor Jesus describes.

LOVE IS NOT EASILY ANGERED

Jack was a mystery. Not really, but it was easier to think of him as a mystery than a bully. He was a warm, smart, and fun-loving friend who could explode at the turn of a phrase. Do you know anyone like Jack?

His anger grew on me, kind of like an old truck I owned that overheated sometimes: it was frustrating, but I learned to deal with it. But then I read a quote that stopped me in my tracks: "Whatever you allow is what will continue." Jack's anger wasn't getting better. I was more and more apprehensive to engage in anything beyond surface cordiality. I noticed others either striving to affirm him, seeking to avoid him, or shutting down around him.

Over coffee one afternoon I asked him how things were going at work and home. He quickly assured me everything was "better than ever." But then the dance I had witnessed over and over began: he leaned in, his eyes widened, his forehead furrowed. With a slightly elevated volume and veiled confrontational tone, he snipped, "Why do you ask?"

Press pause . . . My friend Jack wasn't facing a new struggle. And the apostle Paul's warning that love is not easily angered was not new for the Corinthians either. The Bible is not short on blunt warnings about short-fused folks.

> Fools show their annoyance at once, but the prudent overlook an insult. (Prov. 12:16)
>
> A quick-tempered person does foolish things. (Prov. 14:17a)
>
> Whoever is patient has great understanding, but one who is quick-tempered displays folly. (Prov. 14:29)
>
> Do not make friends with a hot-tempered person, do not associate with one easily angered, or you may learn their ways and get yourself ensnared. (Prov. 22:24–25)

I realized over time that Jack did not see himself as an easily-angered. When his facially contorted reactions invited others to engage in an aggressive interaction, they normally just backed down, and away. But Jack interpreted this to be *their* deficiency. He always had an answer and was sure *his answer was always right*. People quickly learned, as one of his co-workers confided, "The stress of any disagreement with him just isn't worth it."

What was going on with Jack?

I believe part of Jack's challenge was honesty. That may seem like a strange response, and I know he would not accept my assessment— at least at first. It would be very difficult for Jack to say something like, "I don't feel compelled to ask others for their true feedback on my interactions because I trust my own intuitions about life more than what others think." In other words, "I'm smarter about life than you, and if you have a problem with me, that's on you."

The Corinthian Christians were like Jack. They would be the last to acknowledge that their way of interacting with each other was not healthy. One of their mottos, quoted three times by Paul, was "Everything is permissible." This was their way of saying, "Whatever we think is right, *is* right." A second less-known quote that is actually more telling is found in 1 Corinthians 6:13, "Food for the stomach and the stomach for food." This is a proverbial way of saying, "If I feel like doing something, then it's okay." It is no surprise that the Corinthian church seized on the sexual implication of this proverb, but it has a much broader application. This "permissive" way of thinking gave them permission to do what they felt like doing and reject any suggestion that they might be wrong.

Love and angry outbursts are not meant to go together. Do you remember the "jack-in-the-box toy? That creepy music filling you with anxious anticipation! According to folklore, *this was no toy* back in the fourteenth century when Englishman Sir John Schorne became the original Ghostbuster. He is often pictured holding a boot in which he had captured a devil that he had exorcised in protecting the village of North Marston in Buckinghamshire. The French version is literally called a "boxed devil." In 1951 Mattel manufactured the first musical jack-in-the-box and called it "Jolly Tune the Clown," which those who hate clowns might think is a perfect translation of *boxed devil*! In 1971, Mattel finally arrived at the iconic friendly "jack" we know today.

You might have an angry *Jack*-in-the-box in your life, like my friend I described earlier. But I must confess to being an easily angered person in my younger years. My wife and I had been married about four years when in anger I punched my fist through the wall in our home. As I type these words now, the original event seems like another lifetime. But what followed my outburst was an interesting counseling session and support group. I was a young minister in a small town, so I received a referral to a Christian counseling center about an hour away. I went in for my appointment. I had to get past being so easily angered.

The psychologist helped me talk about what happened and why. I appreciated the progress and felt better when I left. On my second visit, we dug a little deeper. He asked me if I thought my wife should join us, since my fit of rage was a response to something she had said. I told him, "No, I don't think my wife should come with me. I was like this before I met her, so I know it is not *her* problem." I then asked him, "What does a person with a short fuse do?" He replied, "Get a longer fuse." He then charged me sixty-five dollars. I thought to myself, "Are you kidding? You just charged me the full rate for that?"

"What does a person with a short fuse do?"

I went back the next week, and he suggested that I join an anger-management support group for several weeks to gain insight and to experience mutual encouragement. He gave me the address. I went to the group. There were five of us. The other four were postal workers. *True story*! This was 1986. Go google "going postal" and check this out. I had to appreciate the irony. I was supposed to represent the King of Peace, and here I was going postal.

I don't mean to demean postal workers or preachers, but I want to emphasize the truth that the love-condition of not being easily angered doesn't apply just to people outside the church. The church itself can behave like a jack-in-the-box. We play a friendly tune, offering a sense of care, safety, and compassion until someone turns our crank one too many times, and then they might experience the boxed devil. I've witnessed outbursts regarding politics, culture clashes, and disagreements over how the church should worship. We preach love until someone offends us, and then we pop off with angry outbursts that are no different than anything we would see in politics or on an episode of Jerry Springer.

When we read the account of the murder of Stephen in Acts 7, it is both unsettling and inspiring. The members of the Sanhedrin react to Stephen's preaching with a fit of rage. They are short-fused and easily angered. Stephen is the startling opposite. His

Christ-conditioned response, "Forgive them," is almost an exact quote of Jesus on the cross. One cannot help but wonder how many times Saul (later the converted Paul) replayed the sound of Stephen's voice in his head. Did Paul's chest tighten up when he thought back to the explosion of anger that crushed the life out of Stephen? When his hand gripped the quill and he wrote, "Love is not easily angered," did his fingers shake? Paul knew the deadly force of unrestrained rage.

We see it today. In the aftermath of racial tensions in cities like Ferguson, Baltimore, Baton Rouge, Minneapolis, Dallas, and others. It is easy to look at the looting and burning of businesses and then use these outbursts as *scapegoats* for our own quick temper. We might even think of ourselves as superior, since "we are not like them." When we cringe at the horrific violence of ISIS or the terrorist attacks in Paris, Nice, Brussels, London, Baghdad, Kabul, Nairobi, Madrid, or Istanbul, we again can easily place our sins on their heads. When we peel back the truth about unhealthy anger, it keeps getting closer and closer to home.

We see it in road rage. Consider the case of Gary L. Durham. He was shot to death during a road-rage incident on July 10, 2016. That was after he had served more than a decade in prison for killing a man . . . in a road-rage dispute in 2001.

We see it in domestic violence. The research on domestic violence is often ignored by Christians because they don't believe it is a large problem in the church. This is why *Christianity Today* reported on domestic violence in churches under the title "The Silent Epidemic." The domestic violence highlighted in the CT report is corroborated by multiple studies:

- According to a UN report in 2007, "Globally, women between the ages of 15–44 are more likely to be maimed or die as the result of male violence than through cancer, malaria, traffic accidents, or war *combined*."

- Amnesty International reported that "on average there have been 35 assaults before a victim of domestic abuse calls the police."
- The FBI reported that "the number of American women who were murdered by current or ex-male partners between 2001 and 2012 was slightly less than double the number of American troops killed in Afghanistan and Iraq during that same time period."
- The World Health Organization reported in 2013 that "35% of women around the globe have experienced sexual or physical abuse by a partner or non-partner."
- The U.S. Center for Disease Control also revealed in their research that the chance of a male experiencing abuse at the hand of an intimate partner was one in seven, and from 2003 to 2015, 18,000 women were killed by men in domestic violence disputes.
- IMA World Health reported on a study conducted by LifeWay Research that surveyed pastors and churches in response to domestic abuse. They found that 65 percent of pastors have spoken one or fewer times about domestic and sexual violence, with only 22 percent reporting that they even addressed it annually. Thirty-three percent of the pastors said they mentioned it rarely and 10 percent said they had never taught on it. Why? The pastors noted that they "did not see sexual or domestic violence as central to larger religious themes such as strong families, a peaceful society, pursuing holiness, and social justice." Yet it is estimated that the percentage of Christians affected by domestic abuse is similar to those who do not claim to be Christian.[1]

Another painful, but important statistic embedded in this research is that "worldwide, men who were exposed to domestic violence as children are three to four times more likely to perpetrate violence as adults than men who did not experience domestic abuse as children."[2]

What is happening here? Is it possible that our society is perpetuating violence and the church has become an accomplice? The violence I am suggesting is both internal and external to the church. One expression of this violence is the *un*conditioned anger, rage, malice, and slander that Christians heap on other Christians. I have been appalled at the permission Christians give themselves to "bite and devour" others by what they post, re-post, and "like" on social media. I believe the apostle Paul would ask us, and he did ask the Corinthians, "And you do this in plain sight of unbelievers?" The church is losing traction in our society primarily because of our *un*conditioned love. People are no longer willing to listen to our pleasant song, only to have the boxed devil pop out!

The impact of easily angered Christians is hard to reverse, and it is not just road rage, race-related tension, or domestic violence. One of the "jack-in-the-box" triggers for the Western church is how to live faithfully in relationship with our friends and family who are gay. This question can evoke stunning compassion and striking brutality. Some Christians avoid the subject like they avoid gay people, while others engage, but end up inflicting unconscionable damage. But what if a church was courageous enough to engage in serious Bible study *and* Christ-conditioned love? What might that church look like as it reaches out and embraces their gay neighbors? Hillsong Church, though not claiming anywhere to have it all together, offers a meaningful example of what it looks like to hold faithfully to what they believe is biblical while not being easily angered or offended.

Their doctrine in regard to marriage is closely aligned to the orthodox view of one man and one woman. Though they welcome gay people, including gay couples to be members of their church, they do not affirm gay sexual relationships as acceptable according to the Bible. This is not a popular position in today's culture. So why aren't the millennials pounding this church with criticism or abandoning the church in protest? The answer seems straighforward: the attitude of the church is humble, transparent, kind, patient, and bathed in love. They live what they believe to be true, but in an environment conditioned by love. When same-sex couples come to their church, they are welcomed with love, respect, and dignity. Absent are the wagging tongues, cruel criticisms, glaring looks and malicious gossips. They have decided to love first.

Christians often use phrases like, "I was offended by . . ." or "They are so offensive" in order to justify their angry responses toward individuals and society. This is a way of blaming someone else for our easily provoked anger. In his book, *Unoffendable*, Brant Hansen delivers a tough teaching. He challenges the angry demeanor of Christians and gives no wiggle room.

> We humans are experts at casting ourselves as victims and rewriting narratives that put us in the center of injustices. And we can repaint our anger or hatred of someone—say, anyone who threatens us—into a righteous-looking work of art. And yet, remarkably, in Jesus's teaching, there is no allowance for "Okay, well, if someone really *is* a jerk, then yeah—you need to be offended." We're flat-out told to *forgive*, even—especially!—the very stuff that's understandably maddening and legitimately offensive. That's the whole point: *The thing that you think makes your anger "righteous" is the very thing that you are called to forgive.* Grace isn't for the deserving. Forgiving means surrendering your claim to resentment and letting go of anger.

"You must not harbor anger. Even when attacked we should love our enemies."

> Anger is extraordinarily easy. It's our default setting. Love is very difficult. Love is a miracle."[3]

As Martin Luther King Jr. once said: "You must not harbor anger. Even when attacked we should love our enemies."[4]

Love-First Reflections

- Does it surprise you that Christ-conditioned love is not easily angered? Why or why not?

- Have you ever regretted expressing your anger?

- Have you ever regretted restraining your anger?

- Why is it easier to unleash our anger over social media?

- Fill in the blanks:

 "The thing that you think makes your anger ___________ is the very thing that you are called to _______________."

 "Grace isn't for the _________________."

 "Anger is extraordinarily _________________. Love is very ___________."

LOVE KEEPS NO RECORD OF WRONGS

> *"Do not seek revenge or bear a grudge against anyone among your people, but love your neighbor as yourself. I am the Lord. Keep my decrees." (Lev. 19:18–19)*

"God gave you a memory. It's a great tool, and he expects you to use it well. You can't control everything that goes into your memory. Sometimes you will hear and see things that you wish never got into your mind, but it's there now, and you have to know what to do with it. Think of your memory like a car. You can't do anything about all those memories in the car, but you know some of them do not belong in the driver's seat. They will fight you for control, but you have to put them back in their place, and that takes work." This was my dad's answer when I asked him how he forgave others and kept from holding grudges against people who had betrayed him or done evil toward him. Memory and forgiveness do go together, but it is important to clarify how. What does it mean that love keeps no record of wrongs?

I've heard preachers thunder from the pulpit, "If you don't forget, you have not forgiven!" But after a cover-to-cover search of Scripture, I found that never once is *forgetting* required as a condition of forgiving. Let me repeat that: Nowhere in the Bible are humans commanded to forgive *and* forget. Consider a simple yet pragmatic question: "*If you could forget, what would there be to forgive*?"

Forgiveness is the act of offering restoration or a relationship where we absolutely remember the sin that caused the wound in the first place. This is the kind of orgiveness that is illustrated when the Old Testament prophet Hosea, who represents God in the story, is called to forgive his wife Gomer after her adultery. Hosea knows and remembers everything she has done to him, and yet he loves and forgives. We see this forgiveness modeled by Jesus when he restores Peter following his resurrection (John 21). There was no indication that Jesus had spiritual amnesia. The sting of Peter's betrayal was still fresh in Jesus's mind, and Peter knew it. But this was the key: *The power in Jesus's forgiveness was the undeniable reality of Peter's denials.*

A brief linguistic reference probably is in order here because you may be thinking about verses that proclaim God's willingness to "remember our sins no more." First, if God has a way of erasing his eternal, omniscient memory, that's awesome for him. But it appears, by the words he uses both in Hebrew and Greek that he is simply suggesting that in the eternal accounting system, *sins forgiven are debts covered.* Our sins are no longer posted to our account.

Remember that Jesus is the Lamb slain before the creation of the world. This means that God knew of our sins even before we committed them, so it shouldn't be surprising that he *can* remember every sin we've ever committed. But herein is the miracle of his forgiveness: he knows our sin *and* chooses not to keep a record. So in 1 Corinthians 13:5, Christ-conditioned love chooses to drop the charges, to cancel the debt, to reckon all things settled.

This condition of love takes a decided turn toward the difficult when we get to the last word: "Love keeps no record of *wrongs*." The word translated here means to keep no record of *being harmed, injured, sinned against, treated wrongly, evil*. All these words are awful, but the last one really stings. It means that when someone loves me Christ's way, they are not recording against me the evil I've done. *But I don't like my missteps to be called "evil."* I am more willing to think of the wrongs of others as evil, but I am more generous in judgment toward myself. But Scripture is clear that we all do evil. Romans 3:9–18, 23 leaves no one out when it comes to sin, and Paul uses the word "evil" to describe *his own* struggle (Rom. 7:19–20). When we keep a record of wrongs it is as if evil wins a double victory: we are wounded by the original offense and in turn we repay the wound by holding a grudge. Love intends to bless. Evil intends to harm. When we keep a record of wrongs, we multiply the harm that evil can accomplish. Forgiveness is the crown jewel of true love. No amount of rehearsing past sins or revenge will make things right. Forgiveness is our only hope for victory over evil. Consider Paul's description of the victorious power of sincere love:

> Love must be sincere. Hate what is *evil*; cling to what is good. Be devoted to one another in love. Bless those who persecute you; bless and do not curse. Do not repay anyone *evil* for *evil*. Be careful to do what is right in the eyes of everyone. If it is possible, as far as it depends on you, live at peace with everyone. Do not take revenge, my dear friends, but leave room for God's wrath, for it is written: "It is mine to avenge; I will repay," says the Lord. On the contrary: "If your enemy is hungry, feed him; if he is thirsty, give him something to drink. In doing this, you will heap burning coals on his head." *Do not*

> *be overcome by evil, but overcome evil with good.* (Rom. 12:9–10a, 14, 17–21)
>
> . . . and whatever other command there may be, are summed up in this one command: "Love your neighbor as yourself." Love does no harm [evil] to a neighbor. Therefore love is the fulfillment of the law. (Rom. 13:9b–10, emphasis mine)

Love does no evil to others even if evil has been done to you. This is a very difficult condition to accept. Proverbs 14:16 reveals that our natural inclination will fight against this Christian command. "The wise fear the LORD and shun evil, but a fool is hotheaded and yet feels secure." It is more "normal" to be hotheaded toward the person that did me wrong, and then to feel completely justified. Eye-for-an-eye makes sense. Worldly logic says to even the score by treating someone as badly as they treated me, but the Spirit of God calls us to live above the savagery of revenge.

> You have heard that it was said, "Eye for eye, and tooth for tooth." But I tell you, do not resist an *evil* person. If anyone slaps you on the right cheek, turn to them the other cheek also. You have heard that it was said, "Love your neighbor and hate your enemy." But I tell you, love your enemies and pray for those who persecute you, that you may be children of your Father in heaven. (Matt. 5:38–39, 43-45a, emphasis mine)

No passage makes clearer the connection between divine love and responding to the evil that people do. What does Jesus have to do for us to embrace his Love-First orthodoxy? This is fundamentally the problem with the love-less creeds of Christian history. It cannot be said enough: We live by our creeds, written or unwritten. And since not one of our ancient Christian creeds even mentions the word *love*, it should not surprise us that our history is littered with eye-for-an-eye reactions to the evil (real and perceived) that Christians have endured.

While on the cross, Jesus did not disconnect from his earlier teaching about love. Of his seven utterances on Calvary, "Father, forgive them, for they know not what they do" may be the most crucial model Christians need to reclaim today. The world must see the power of the cross played out in real life—in our lives.

Betsie and Corrie ten Boom

Casper ten Boom was a watchmaker in Holland. During WWII and the Nazi occupation of the Netherlands, the ten Boom family home became "the hiding place" for Jews. On February 28, 1944, a Dutch informant tipped off the Nazis. In all, around thirty members of the ten Boom family were arrested. Within ten days of his arrest, Casper died in a Nazi prison. Betsie, Casper's eldest daughter, died in the Ravensbruck concentration camp on December 16, 1944. Corrie, Betsie's youngest sister survived the war and returned to the Netherlands, where she set up a rehabilitation center for war refugees. She also sheltered the jobless Dutch who had previously collaborated with the Germans during the occupation—the very people who had betrayed her family in the first place.

At the Holocaust memorial complex in Jerusalem, Yad Vashem, Casper, Betsie, and Corrie are honored in the Garden of the Righteous for their repeated and substantial assistance to help the Jews during that awful time. When I was visiting Yad Vashem with my family, it struck me that the ten Booms and people like them should be held in the highest honor among Christians as well—the *righteous among us*. I simply cannot get over Corrie's later love and forgiveness of those who cost her so much, including her beloved father and sister. She demonstrated the truth that love keeps no record of evil.

Out of her experience with the gospel in the midst of such evil, Corrie wrote,

> Forgiveness is an act of the will, and the will can function regardless of the temperature of the heart. Even as the angry vengeful thoughts boiled through me, I saw the sin of them [of her own thoughts]. Jesus Christ had died for this man; was I going to ask for more? Lord Jesus, I prayed, forgive me and help me to forgive him. . . . Jesus, I cannot forgive him. Give me your forgiveness. . . . And so I discovered that it is not on our forgiveness any more than on our goodness that the world's healing hinges, but on His. When He tells us to love our enemies, He gives along with the command, the love itself.[1]

Not a Broken Record . . . But No Record at All!

It is doubtful that any contemporary national figure was *more* committed to a core of compassionate forgiveness than Martin Luther King Jr. It was both his Christian conviction and his foundational philosophy for social change. But when King wrote and spoke, he combined forgiveness with the themes of justice and love. In one sermon he insisted, "We must develop and maintain the capacity to forgive. He who is devoid of the power to forgive is devoid of the power to love. There is some good in the worst of us and some evil in the best of us. When we discover this, we are less prone to hate our enemies."[2] As King continued this sermon, he reflected on Jesus's pattern of comprehensive forgiveness.

> [For Jesus,] forgiveness is more than an occasional act, but it is a permanent attitude. And he talked about love: "Love your enemies. Bless them that curse you. Pray for them that despitefully use you." . . . They had been taught to seek redress in the time-honored tradition of retaliation. But he continued to talk about love and forgiveness. . . And we must never forget that Jesus was

> nailed to the cross not merely because of human badness but because of human blindness.[3]

These inspiring examples call us to an intelligent and disciplined approach to keeping no record of wrongs. When we recall a wrong, in that moment we must decide which way our memory will bend. Will we nudge the trajectory toward the long arc of forgiveness and love, or will we enter the same wounds again as if that exact wound has, by our memory of it, been inflicted by the original perpetrator again.

If we choose the path of forgiveness, we will find ourselves better armed for the fight against resentment. Notice the word *re-sent-ment*. This word comes from the meaning "take ill; be in some degree angry or to be provoked." If we choose to keep *re-sending* the wrongs of others to the debit ledger, we build a permanent case against ourselves. *Yes, ourselves.* Jesus warned that *he will judge us as we judge others.* The measure we use against others will be used against us. It is like two cases being tried in different courts but at the same time. As we mount evidence against another person, casting them before the court as hopelessly deserving destruction, are we not, according to Jesus, making the same case against ourselves in the heavenly court? His words are clear:

> If you forgive other people when they sin against you, your heavenly Father will also forgive you. But if you do not forgive others their sins, your Father will not forgive your sins. (Matt. 6:14–15)
>
> Do not judge, or you too will be judged. For in the same way you judge others, you will be judged, and with the measure you use, it will be measured to you. (Matt. 7:1–5)

One of Jesus's most famous parables on forgiveness began when Peter asked how much is too much when we are called upon to forgive another. Our Lord's famous reply of "seventy times seven" wasn't meant to be treated as a math problem, but as a relational solution. The only condition placed on forgiveness is that it be driven by the love we have received from God.

This parable sets up a greater/lesser dichotomy, common to the teachers of Jesus's time. In the story, a person who owes more than the national debt is forgiven, only to turn around and choke the life out of a fellow servant who is three months behind on his rent. When the master hears about this, he reinstates the burden of full repayment on the first servant, essentially giving him life in prison. This story has some rough edges to it, but the final line is the one Jesus wants us to get: "This is how my heavenly Father will treat each of you unless you forgive your brother or sister from your heart" (Matt. 18:35).

Without the lengthy parable, Jesus's brother James delivers a blunt message that when we judge each other in slanderous ways, we are actually judging God and his law. And as his readers know, James doesn't mince words. "Brothers and sisters, do not slander one another," he commands. And then he explains why. "Anyone who speaks against a brother or sister or judges them speaks against the law and judges it. . . . Who are you to judge your neighbor?" (4:11–12).

It turns out that justice and judgment are not the same thing. Justice is the value that should govern our judgment. Jesus taught us to do unto others what we would have them do to us. This is an expression of justice. It is a fulfillment of Micah 6:8. Love and justice are teammates, while love and judgmentalism are adversaries.

Just before Jesus delivers the Golden Rule, he commands us not to judge each other. Why do we keep a record of the wrongs of others, especially when Jesus tells us that every time we record one of their sins in our ledger, he records ours in his? Jesus even names the ledgers: the one we keep of others he calls "Splinters," and the one being kept of us is called "Logs." Only Christ-conditioned love can empower us to quit writing in the Book of Splinters and turn our lives into letters of love. Keeping no record of wrongs means forgiving others in light of the immeasurable forgiveness given us in Christ Jesus. Forgive is an act of justice; it is doing for others what God is doing for us.

In our current social and political turmoil, the temptation to abandon the Love-First Christ-creed has never been more alluring. At every level we are desperate for examples of Christ followers who will forgive and love rather than repay evil for evil. We must purge our files of the sins we hold against others and ourselves. Forgiveness deletes the spiritual malware in our hearts and minds, allowing the Spirit of God full access to our operating system. This is God's plan for ending hate before it's too late.

Love-First Reflections

- In what way did Jesus set the bar for "keeping no record of wrongs"?

- In Corrie ten Boom's quote and prayer she says, "Jesus Christ had died for this man; was I going to ask for more? 'Lord Jesus, forgive me and help me to forgive him . . .' And so I discovered that it is not on our forgiveness any more than on our goodness that the world's healing hinges." How does acknowledging Christ's forgiveness for your own sins lead you to forgiving someone else? Could anything more be paid to cancel out the cumulative sins of the world?

- Why did Martin Luther King Jr. say the cross was not merely because of our badness, but also because of our blindness? To what do you believe we are blind?

- Read Matthew 7:1–5, 12 and Matthew 22:37–40. Why do you suppose Jesus followed his teaching on "not judging" just a few verses later with the Golden Rule?

- How does the Golden Rule influence how you understand Paul's teaching that love keeps no record of wrongs?

16

LOVE DOES NOT DELIGHT IN INJUSTICE

When reviewing the verdict of a court, we often give our opinion as to whether "justice was served." When I was younger, I mistakenly thought that meant, "Was the proper penalty handed out?" But justice being served actually means, "Did justice have its way in the process of law? Was justice held up as the standard to which the proceedings were held accountable?" In essence, did justice or injustice win? When justice loses its supremacy, people become victims of injustice.

But here is another point of confusion: law and justice are not the same. This is why we speak of "unjust laws." In fact, in the history of many nations, great heroes broke unjust laws to bring about justice. We think of the American Revolution, the civil rights movement, those who mounted internal resistance against Hitler, and so many more. Let their words echo over you.

> "Justice will not be served until those who are unaffected are as outraged as those who are." —*Benjamin Franklin*

"The arc of the moral universe is long, but it bends towards justice." —*Martin Luther King Jr.*

"We are not to simply bandage the wounds of victims beneath the wheels of injustice, we are to drive a spoke into the wheel itself." —*Dietrich Bonhoeffer*

"Never forget that justice is what love looks like in public." —*Cornel West*

The Witness

Our commitment to knowing God finds strength, guidance, and nourishment in the Scriptures. When the Spirit moves me to seek God's will more fully in a particular area, I begin by praying for an open heart and a fervent desire to learn from him. My next move is to open the Word of God. I compiled a list of every narrative, psalm, teaching, or command in Scripture that speaks to what the Spirit is laying on my heart. As I considered what it means to live justly, I discovered a mighty river rolling through Scripture that linked love and justice. Scripture roots justice in the very nature of God and calls us to live justly as a witness to God's presence and purpose in the world.[1]

Justice Is Non-negotiable

Embedded in the Christ-conditions of love is the value of justice. In Jesus's teachings, truth isn't about being right (as in winning an argument); instead, truth is a defining characteristic of life. He is the truth. He is full of grace and truth. All who worship him worship "in Spirit and in truth." His disciples will know the truth and it will set them free. All who are on the side of truth, side with Jesus. For Jesus, truth is not simply a verifiable fact; but rather, truth is a way of living rightly and justly with everyone.

In the case of the Pharisees, Jesus rarely disagreed with the *factuality* of their teachings, but he exposed them for not living the truth. Jesus linked living the truth with justice and love. "Woe to you Pharisees," he scolded them, "because you give God a tenth of your mint, rue, and all other kinds of garden herbs, but you neglect justice and the love of God. You should have practiced the latter without leaving the former undone" (Luke 11:42). These Pharisees were the experts in the Law of God, but they neglected justice and the love of God. They didn't like his teaching because he insisted on Love-First, and everything they were doing was being measured and found lacking by this non-negotiable priority of Jesus.

It seems strange that Paul would warn the Corinthians not to rejoice when evil is happening. But this Greek word translated *evil* is the word for "unrighteousness" or "injustice." The apostle Paul wrote, "Love is never glad when others go wrong." All the conditions of love articulated so far are the backdrop for this final "negative" condition of love. If one is envious, proud, self-seeking, and keeps a record of wrongs, then when another is vulnerable, this *un*conditioned Christian will actually take delight in the failures of others. Though it may be fleeting, we can feel a sense of superiority when we hasten the demise of another person, especially if we already don't like them. Those who belittled, demeaned, brutalized, and killed Jesus displayed their false superiority as they mocked him and took delight in his death. Those who rejoice in the downfall of others are spiritual descendants of Christ's persecutors.

When I was a young man, I had many vices and I left a trail of shameful behavior. As I grew and matured in Christ after my college years, I suffered internally with shame. Every time someone brought up my past to put me down, my soul would shrink. I discovered three consistent "qualities" in those who use the pain of our past to do us harm in the present:

- The facts are not important. Alternative facts are just fine with them, and even verified evidence to the contrary will rarely turn them around.

- They find some level of satisfaction in landing a painful blow.
- Only a few have the courage and Spirit-led humility to go back and make a good-faith attempt to heal the damage they have already done when they discover their information or perceptions were wrong.

Why would we hope that someone will be ruined? Why do we revel in the downfall of others? Some helpful psychological studies provide insight into this component of human behavior—from microaggression to macro-destruction—but from the biblical perspective, the answer is simple: *injustice grows in the love-starved soil of the human heart.*

Conditioned by Categories

Our brains are part of this equation. At the core of our cognitive equipment is a categorization mechanism that guides our lives. This capacity for categories is essential to our survival and efficiency. This is how we determine safety from danger, fresh from rotten, warm from scalding, exciting from threatening. As children, we learn snaps from buttons, Velcro from laces, bees from butterflies. As we mature, we learn to discern critique from belittlement, anger from rage, disagreement from belligerence, leadership from tyranny. This is also how we develop doctrine.

The doctrines we live in our personal lives and in our churches are a form of categorization. In seminary we even have required studies called "Systematic Theology." Our systems of doctrine form categories of churches. We broadly speak about Protestant, Evangelical, Catholic, Orthodox, Pentecostal, and non-denominational churches. And this makes sense because of the way our brains work.

When we categorize, we also prioritize, and this is natural. For example, if we are chasing a piece of paper blowing in the wind and it swooshes out in front of a speeding truck, our priority instantly shifts from catching the paper to avoiding the truck. Our lives depend on this form of prioritization. Having the correct priority in the moment is literally a matter of life or death.

But cognitive categorization carries a stern warning label: "Danger! Categorization of humans may cause irreversible destruction." When we human beings categorize other human beings as "different," we quickly consider them less than us. Even when "different" is wrapped around a disability, we often love others more with pity than with respect. This negative categorization of people can lead to abuse and death, but most of the time we do not recognize in our words and actions the potential for destruction.

I was preparing for a college course I taught for several years on the Gospel of John. As I was looking closely at the familiar story in 8:1–11—the one about the woman caught committing adultery—I had three successive epiphanies:

1. In verse 6, the narrator of the story gives an important observation.
2. Jesus treats the accusers with the same grace he offers the woman.
3. Jesus's life is a living parable.

Let's take these in order. First, try to read the story without verse 6. Notice how it flows? If verse 6 wasn't in the story, you might never know the difference, but for the Gospel of John, this verse is the key. It is like John steps into the role of narrator to clue us in on why these men dragged this woman out of her bed of shame into public condemnation. *They were using her to get to Jesus*. They needed to ambush him so that he would make a mistake. Their plan was to catch him in a double bind: no matter what he said, they were sure they could build a case against him. If he supported her death, he was not full of grace. If he supported her life, he was not full of truth. The whole issue surrounded the word in our English translations, "accuse." They needed a way to discredit him, and since he wasn't guilty of sin, they had to use accusations to turn the crowds against him.

The Greek word behind our word *accuse* is the verb *kategoreo*. There are two noun forms; *kategoria* that translates as accusation(s), and *kategoros* that refers to the accuser(s). If we look closely at this word cluster, or better yet, if we read them aloud, we will see or hear our English word *category*. This turns out to be more than verbal trivia. This is like cracking a secret code. In Revelation 12:10, Satan is called the *kategor*. He is the accuser. Accusations function far beyond charges, evidence, or conviction. Accusations categorize people, and it is much easier to justify certain actions if we bypass personal interaction and move straight to categories. Let me illustrate:

- If someone is in prison we categorize them as criminals and assume they are more violent than those who are on the outside. But is this really the truth?
- When I was young, if a girl "got pregnant," she was viewed differently in church circles than the boys and girls who were having sex but didn't get pregnant. Stories about "those kinds of girls" often dogged them into their adult lives.
- One of our sons is an African-American. The skin he's wrapped in is darker than that of his siblings. During his late teens he was pulled over by the police three different times. He was searched and cuffed, but given *no citations*. He was, however, chastised by the officers for being in a part of town "where he didn't belong."
- On a global scale, humanity's capacity for categorical evil has been on display in the slave trade, the Holocaust, apartheid, the Rwandan genocide, Jim Crow laws, violence against the LGBTQ community, sex trafficking . . .

> The list could go on forever. There is no era in recorded history when a culture was exempt from violence rooted in the negative categorization of a people group.

When Satan, the *kategor*, categorized Jesus as a danger to the Jews and the Romans, his brutal death was sealed. This is the outcome we have come to expect in lynchings, nightclub massacres, suicide bombings, and racially targeted violence. Negative categorization is Satan's most effective weapon of mass destruction, accounting for the abuse, enslavement, and slaughter of millions in human history.

Let's return to the story of the woman caught in adultery.

The mob got her sin right, but got themselves wrong. There were not two categories of people: the righteous represented by them, and the disgusting sinners represented by her. They were all one. They were *people who sinned*, and she was a *person who sinned*. Jesus encouraged them to see themselves as the target—the sinners at whom the stones were aimed—and then to see if they still agreed that this was the best way to approach a sinner.

The Bible says that the older guys dropped their rocks and walked away first. John offers no commentary on why they left first, but I am certain that when the seasoned veterans in the group acknowledged their sin-solidarity with the woman, the vein-pulsing passion for her blood drained out of the young men as well. Who knows but that the men recognized their own arousal as they pulled her from the bed? Maybe their self-righteous crusade to destroy Jesus was now mixed with their own boiling sexual aggression. They could not think. Their cognitive abilities were paralyzed by their categorically permitted rage. As soon as Jesus exposed their shared humanity with the woman, they lost their will to destroy one of their own—the woman.

Jesus then did for the woman the same thing he did for her accusers. He restored her humanity, releasing her from the prison of categorization. The men no longer accused her, Jesus no longer accused her. The last accuser left was herself. Jesus let her know that her past was not the best indicator of future behavior. She was not categorically doomed to a future of immorality and adultery. She could move forward toward a life of righteousness with bold confidence.

If we are to end hate before it's too late, we must focus the mighty energy of love on turning the wheels of justice until all God's children are equally protected from those who would destroy their lives by attack or neglect.

If we are to end hate before it's too late, we must focus the mighty energy of love on turning the wheels of justice until all God's children are equally protected from those who would destroy their lives by attack or neglect. This last item on Paul's list of love descriptions in 1 Corinthians 13 is the only one on the list where Paul adds the orthodoxy option: instead of cheering when others go down, what if we reserve our rejoicing for when truth wins out?

Words that Turn the Wheel and Heal

Should you say everything you could say? My dad suggested otherwise: "Normally your first thought is not your best thought. Not everything you think is right, but even if it is, it may not be good, wise, or loving of you to say it." We often overestimate our ability to formulate truth. We get caught up in fake news and alternative facts. Then our lies are hard to abandon because we have used them to construct our truth. I have known many people who formulated their opinions of others with bits of information. They lack the courage to go through the necessary steps to arrive at real truth, immersed in love and the Golden Rule. Since they are not committed to Christ-conditioned love, they then share their opinions as facts and divorce themselves from the downstream consequences of their words.

Many of the vocal Pharisees in Jesus's day were more than willing to speak about him in a way that sullied his reputation and cast suspicion on his motives. They decided that Jesus was loose with the truth, not committed to the traditions handed down by the elders, and a threat to their orthodoxy. They rejoiced in the evil of his crucifixion because they saw it as a win. He got what they believed he deserved . . . justice. But everything they did to Jesus with their words was unjust. The way they treated him, the outcome of their smear campaign, and the lack of remorse for their actions are a pure and painful example of rejoicing in evil.

But not all the Pharisees were like this. Nicodemus is a faith-thread in the Gospel of John. He comes to Jesus first at night, the lone emissary of the "we" among whom he has been discussing Jesus. He wants to know who Jesus is and what his life means. We do not hear of Nicodemus again until chapter 7. The religious rulers have decided to do Jesus in. He has to go. And once you decide someone has to go, you can do whatever you want to him. They send officers to arrest him. They come back impressed by him. The leaders are furious. Let's pick up the story here:

> "You mean he has deceived you also?" the Pharisees retorted. "Have any of the rulers or of the Pharisees believed in him? No! But this mob that knows nothing of the law—there is a curse on them."
>
> Nicodemus, who had gone to Jesus earlier and who was one of their own number, asked, "Does our law condemn a man without first hearing him to find out what he has been doing?"
>
> They replied, "Are you from Galilee, too? Look into it, and you will find that a prophet does not come out of Galilee." (7:47–52)

The angry Pharisees are accusatory. They call him names. They suggest that the guards are deceived, the crowds are cursed know-nothings. And when one of their own, Nicodemus, simply suggests following the Law to hear a case before casting a judgment, they humiliate him by insulting his home state. As evil gains momentum, the crowd bcomes a mob. They justify their injustice as a *necessary* evil. But Nicodemus's question must be heard in the light of his first visit to Jesus (3:1–2).

When Nicodemus tells Jesus "we" know you're from God, this "we" is the extra set of ears I want you to listen through when Nicodemus clashes with his colleagues in 7:51. The religious leaders are using bombastic threats and accusations to get the rest of their group to get on board with their rejection of Jesus. But Nicodemus is not alone. He is one of the "we" who seriously desires to live justly and see truth win out. *He represents other silent lovers of justice who do not yet have the social confidence or personal fortitude to speak out.*

All four Gospel accounts record the death and burial of Jesus. Nicodemus is certainly a key character, but we meet another member of the Jewish ruling council who would be silent in the face of injustice no longer. Nicodemus's courage provides an example for Joseph of Arimathea who then boldly steps beyond his fear. Together, they recovered the body of Jesus from the cross, and placed him in a tomb cut in the rocks (John 19:38–40 and Luke 23:50–53).

The progression in this story is undeniable. Nicodemus would not stand by and allow injustice to crush the quiet and silence the questioning. Those who stand for justice are never alone. There is always an unseen cloud of witnesses who simply long for someone with courage to step forward. Nicodemus now comes to us as he first came to Jesus, in the night of our timidity, to remind us that when Christ-conditioned love is boldly lived in the workplace, schools, courts, and churches, *injustice is temporary*, and truth wins out.

Love-First Reflections

- Why did the Pharisees dislike Jesus's teaching?

- Read John 8:1–11. What was unjust in the accusation of the woman caught in adultery?

- The Greek word for accuse is ________________. This is related to what English word? How does this help you understand how evil accusations develop so much dangerous momentum?

- Fill in the blank: "Negative categorization is __________ most effective weapon of mass ________________, accounting for the abuse, enslavement and ____________ of millions in human history."

- In what way do you relate to the story of Nicodemus, and how does he inspire you to make your family, community, church, workplace, or school more just for everyone?

Part 4

LOVE FIRST, ALWAYS, AND NEVER

17

IN THE WORLD, BUT NOT OF THE WORLD

I learned to say, "Yes ma'am," in Arkansas. I learned respect for others in Oregon where I grew up, but the added vocabulary was a Southern addition I picked up while in college. My wife and I moved to the north after college, and the respect was still there, but I had a very insulted woman ask me, "Are you mocking me?" when I called her "ma'am."

As we were moving back down south and settling in Atlanta, we stopped at a gas station in Tennessee. Our son Caleb was nine. The cashier was sweetly Southern, and everything was "shuga-pie," "honey-child," and "bless yur heart." As we were walking back to the car, Caleb asked, "So, is that what they call a Southern accident?"

Culture

During my education, I spent several years studying biblical languages. It became apparent that learning a culture required learning a language, but to learn a language, it was necessary to learn a culture. The members of our church speak more than one language. We call their first language their "heart" language.

The word *culture* has come to mean the "collective customs and achievements of a people." The word is derived from the Latin, *cultura*, which means "a cultivating, agriculture, tilling of the land." Culture refers to everyday existence, shared attitudes, values, social practices, goals, and conventions. Culture takes shape as families and larger social groups express and experience life. And certain conditions must be met for us to feel that our culture is being upheld and respected.

Nations, cities, businesses, sports teams, and churches have a culture to them. Alongside the positive examples, we also see negative, evil, and tragic cultures. In light of mass shootings across America, an Internet search yields such results as:

- America's Culture of Violence
- Gun Control and the American Nightmare of Violence
- Confronting a Culture of Violence
- Fostering a Culture of Violence
- A Culture of Abuse—That's What a Church Can Be
- Priests, Abuse, and the Meltdown of a Culture

The word *culture* can be a way of talking about tribal identity. Through the movie, *End of the Spear*, millions of Americans were introduced to five young missionaries who gave their lives to share the love of Jesus with the Auca Indians in Ecuador in 1950. Of the five, Jim Elliot and Nate Saint were the most widely known. The violence of this reclusive tribe was legendary and the slaughter of these five men was only the latest evidence. But then a miracle occurred.

Family members of the slain missionaries returned to live among the Auca in full forgiveness. They became family with each other. Steve Saint, Nate's son, was raised by his father's killer, Mincaye, who became like a father to him and a grandfather to his children.

In a widely published interview surrounding the release of the movie, Steve and Mincaye shared their story and personal reflections. Mincaye stressed that until they received the gospel of Jesus, their tribal ancestors lived in a culture of violence and death. Theirs was a generational legacy of bloodshed. He spoke of their endless anger. Few Auca ever knew a grandfather because of this culture of death.

When the Auca attacked the mission team, the missionaries had guns to defend themselves, but did not use them. They had already decided on this course of action. They didn't believe they could share Christ with this tribe if they participated in the bloodshed. It would have just been one more episode of the same violent tribal culture. But when they died and their relatives did not retaliate, everything changed. This has played out over and over through Christian history, whether it was the transformation of a nation, tribe, family, or single soul.

The covenantal conditions of Christ have been spelled out in the previous chapters, but now we need to ask, "So what would the culture of my life, my community, my work, my school, and my church become if I determined to live the Love-First creed, with all the conditions Christ gave to define his love?"

Jesus uses his own life, teaching, and conversations to plant and cultivate the seed of his culture in us. And according to the apostle Paul, these are the things God's people *always* do and *never* do. Notice this wording—this is the wording of culture. Here is what makes us us, and here is what we will not ever do. This is what describes us, defines us, delineates us. If you become a citizen of this culture, here are the covenant conditions to which we all ascribe.

The Love-First Church

As we enter the home stretch of this book, I want to update us on where we are so far.

- We are in crisis, but our great crisis is *not* the culture around us. The crisis we squarely face is that we are called by God to love first yet we put nearly everything else in our lives ahead of this God-ordained priority.
- I have the utmost respect for the historic Christian creeds passed down to us both in written or verbal form, but I have deep frustration with the omission of *the* creed that Jesus and his apostles articulated. We must hold ourselves accountable to restore Christ's Love-First creed as the codified core of our faith.
- Love has covenantal conditions. Jesus and his followers did not leave us with an unconditioned view of love. Through the Spirit and the explicit instructions in God's Word we know the conditions that have been laid down for the Love-First creed. The concise and celebrated list of conditions in 1 Corinthians 13 speak to our real-life circumstances. They give us a path forward.

By now you may be thinking, "So what's next? What can we do to end hate before it's too late?" Jesus answers this question from a prayer garden. Read these intimate words from Jesus to his Father about his disciples, including you and me.

> I have given them your word and the world has hated them, for they are not of the world any more than I am of the world. My prayer is not that you take them out of the world but that you protect them from the evil one. They are not of the world, even as I am not of it. Sanctify them by the truth; your word is truth. As you sent me into the world, I have sent them into the world. (John 17:14–18)

In the world, not of the world is the popular "CliffsNotes" for this section of Jesus's prayer. The wording is not exact, but the meaning is. For many, this is the go-to verse when stoking the fires of the *church vs. world* culture wars, but David Mathis, blogger and executive editor for DesiringGod.org, seizes Jesus's true intent when he writes,

> For Jesus, being "not of the world" isn't the destination in these verses *but the starting place*. Jesus is not huddling up the team for another round of Kumbaya, but so that we can run the next play and advance the ball down the field. Jesus is not asking his Father for his disciples to be taken out of the world, but he is praying for them as they are "sent into" the world. . . . So maybe it would serve us better—at least in light of John 17—to revise the popular phrase "*in*, but not *of*" in this way: "not *of*, but *sent into*."[1]

It would serve us better to revise the popular phrase "in, but not of" in this way: "not of, but sent into."

– David Mathis

The call to holiness is not the end but the beginning. Being *not of the world* is the beginning of our work *in the world*. The church is not a culture of fearful isolation but of bold transformation. Rather than running from the world or railing against it, we are racing into it with the amazing story of love that captured our hearts and commissioned our lives. Author Gabe Lyons articulates this challenge in a fresh way:

> To a growing group of believers, the changing religious landscape represents a new chapter in the story God is telling through His people. They see it as a new opportunity to send the Gospel out in fresh and compelling ways. Every generation must face this quandary of how to maintain cultural influence, and in our changing world, the conversation has been resurrected again.[2]

After noting the different unproductive ways that Christians have reacted to culture, Lyons argues for something different—living counterculturally.

> The next generation of Christians aren't separatists, antagonists, or striving to be "relevant." Instead, the next Christians see themselves as salt, preserving agents actively working for restoration in the middle of a decaying culture. They understand that by being restorers they fight against the cultural norms and often flow counter to the cultural tide. Paradoxically . . . it's truly good news to the world. Rather than fighting off culture to protect an insular Christian community, they are fighting for the world to redeem it. This is the essence of being what [author] Tim Keller refers to as "*a counterculture for the common good*."[3]

Salt and Light

Working for restoration in the middle of a decaying culture advances the mission of God in the world. Jesus uses the metaphors of salt and light to describe this kind of ministry from the middle of the mess. Salt is applied to food to "condition" it. Salt that does not condition is worthless. But it must be noted that salt unapplied is as worthless as salt that isn't salty. Salt that is perfectly stored away from the surrounding atmosphere is prepared to do its good work. But it might as well be in a museum if it is not going to have contact with and be absorbed into the food it is meant to condition. Paul uses this metaphor as a way to describe our lives in relation to the world around us:

> Pray for us, too, that God may open a door for our message, so that we may proclaim the mystery of Christ, for which I am in chains. Pray that I may proclaim it clearly, as I should. Be wise in the way you act toward outsiders;

> make the most of every opportunity. Let your conversation be always full of grace, seasoned with salt, so that you may know how to answer everyone. (Col. 4:3–6)

Many have pushed back on this interpretation, suggesting that we are to be "strangers in the world, not being unequally yoked with unbelievers, hating even the garments polluted by the flesh." I agree one hundred percent, but this is a false dichotomy. Neither Paul, Jesus, nor any other New Testament writer is making the case for either holy avoidance of the world or an unholy mission to the world. This is not an either/or, but a both/and. We are to engage wholly with the world and be holy among the people God so fervently loves and so feverishly seeks.

But what does this look like? How do we understand being wholly engaged while holding firm to Christ's holy standard? Again the apostle Paul and the Corinthians are instructive. Their internal church culture is wrapped in pride and position. Those with influence are for and against things that advance them, and this includes giving a pass to a brother who is sexually involved with his father's wife. One might wonder if this *really* was going on in that church. Were the Corinthians genuinely boasting about their "amazing grace" toward this guy's erotic escapades? Apparently so. I have seen equally crazy things.

My wife and I were in ministry just six weeks when one member of our church shot and killed another member in a lovers' triangle. I also remember a church business meeting where, in order to make his point, one brother threw his chair against the wall. On another occasion one woman who had visited our church several times called me and my co-pastor to tell us how wonderfully loving our church was. She had never been loved so well. In fact, she reported, one of our ministry leaders had loved her so well that he went to her home one evening and made love to her. Wow!

What a guy! Needless to say, that necessitated a phone call and a come-to-Jesus meeting.

I'm just trying to illustrate that the Corinthian mess is not a hyperbole nor an outlier. For many, keeping ourselves unstained by the world has come to mean rationalizing our acceptable sins and avoiding the world's unacceptable sins. We make peace with greed but condemn gays. We overlook private porn while decrying public promiscuity. Cutting down others is in, but cussing others out is not. Illegal drug addiction is a no-no, but unchecked consumption of food is a yes-yes. I'm not trying to grind your nerves, but if we are going to impact the world, we must address our unintended, yet witness-damaging hypocrisy.

Paul is careful to clarify this. When he challenges his converts to channel their spiritual energy into holiness, he does not mean for them to disengage from the world *at all*. "I wrote to you in my letter not to associate with sexually immoral people—not at all meaning the people of this world who are immoral, or the greedy and swindlers, or idolaters. *In that case you would have to leave this world*. What business is it of mine to judge those outside the church?" (1 Cor. 5:9–10, 12).

The issue Paul addresses is the false notion that being a churchgoer is an insider life. The only walls between the church and the world are the ones we have erected to the detriment of our mission. Christians should move as fluidly between their time together and their time in the world as the very air they breathe.

Light of the World

Tucked within Jesus's *light of the world* commission are four crucial words, "*that they may see*." What does this imply except that we live out our Christ-conditioned lives in the same "trenches" where our co-workers, friends, and neighbors live? Is this not the confession of the Incarnation in John 1? "The Word became flesh and . . . we have seen his glory."

"*We have seen.*" The three words that describe the experience of God-in-the-flesh provide the foundation for the four words that describe our engagement in the world: "*We have seen*," / "*that they may see.*" Jesus is the light that shines in the darkness. And though the world does not receive him (en masse), he is not deterred, for in the broken, violent, and dark world are those longing for the light. They want something different, but they need to see it, touch it.

Christians who have experienced the Love-First commitment of God become Christ-conditioned followers who live out his creed in every arena of life. This is the revolutionary discipleship Jesus imparted to his first followers. The church is in the world to be the salt and light that condition culture with his Love-First creed. I know this makes sense when we look at the ministry of Jesus, but how is it that the church is not known for living this out in our world?

Castle-dwellers

My co-worker Ken Snell has a way of putting truth into a vignette of insight. He articulates the church's challenge this way:

> Many Christians imagine the church like a castle fortress. The world and all its ills on the outside; only the pure and good safe on the inside. We lower our drawbridge and send our missionaries into the dangerous and unsuspecting world to find souls with godly leanings and rush them back to the castle, stopping just long enough outside the walls to baptize them in the moat! Then, after they rush through the gates into the safety of the new community, the drawbridge is raised, thus closing out another risk-filled foray into the wiles of the world.
>
> But the world that God so loved is still suffering and strangling itself in strife. The poor, needy, and oppressed

> cry out to a God who appears to favor the castle-dwellers. But some insist that the king himself had been born, not in the castle, but among them—in a stable. Surely those inside know the story of their king who lives and suffers outside the walls. "*So Jesus also suffered outside the city gate . . . Let us, then, go to him outside the camp . . .*" (Heb. 13:12–13).[4]

Did God really send Jesus into the world to collect a few tenants for mansions above, leaving the rest to writhe in anguish? This is theological foolishness. As Lesslie Newbigin argues in *The Open Secret*, the entire point of the Incarnation is that God's love lives in and through his church to transform his world. The idea that God has called a people unto himself to serve as salt and light in our world is rarely offensive to non-believers. The offense is when the elect act like they are elite.[5]

If your calling and election by Christ mean anything to you, hit your knees and then hit the streets. Do those who have not yet tangibly experienced the love of God *in their exact context* have to go on wondering in their broken hearts why the saved act like we are entitled, or why the castle-dwellers are so disconnected from their manger-born King?

> If your calling and election by Christ mean anything to you, hit your knees and then hit the streets.

We are transformers. We live as aliens within our culture because we've been called to live the Christ-conditioned life in a sin-conditioned world. We do not align with the powers of the world to advance ourselves. We follow Christ as suffering servants in our culture, not as militants triumphing over culture. It is somewhat in vogue, both within the church and without, to invoke the horrific crimes of the conquistadors and crusaders to make a case against the church. There is no excuse for what happened back then. There is no appropriate response but humble confession of the church's guilt. But my experience tells me that this outrage at the Crusades is often a covert act of scapegoating. We imagine ourselves superior to these proselytizing profligates, but I wonder if we have simply refined our methods so that our crimes can't be traced back to us.

It's not just Christians who are silent or apathetic toward the poor, the displaced, the physically and mentally challenged, the underemployed, or those in deplorable housing. Our church campus is located on the northern perimeter of Atlanta. We are surrounded by neighbors who live in one of the three most affluent counties in the Atlanta metro area. These three counties are packed with churches, including Charles Stanley's First Baptist Atlanta and his son Andy Stanley's North Point Community Church. Our churches, schools, jobs, and healthcare are premier, and yet it is men in these three counties that account for the largest percentage of the "buyers" in the sexploitation crisis in our city. We rank in the top five sex-trafficking cities in the United States, depending on the report you cite, with nearly twelve thousand unique offenders, between three hundred and five hundred new young people between the ages of eleven and fourteen lured into the sex-trade each month, and an annual sex-business income of over three hundred million dollars. Once these children are trafficked the first time, they live an average of less than seven more years. The most painful component of all these reports is that "it happens all around us, often in plain sight."[6]

Sadly, though, as churches and communities assail the crime, degradation and irresponsible lifestyles of the urban blight, it is these same communities that are the largest secret offenders. It is like Isaiah 58 all over again. We are going to church by the thousands, yet our cities are going to hell by the millions.

I want to reiterate that I believe in the body of Christ, the church. I believe that no entity on earth is better positioned, *if conditioned*, to bring an overwhelming renewal of faith, hope, and love to our world. But we must get clear on what our Love-First culture brings to the world when we live in their midst.

Love-First Reflections

- Read John 17:14–19. Referring to David Mathis's quote, fill in the blanks. "Maybe it would serve us better to revise the popular phrase, "in, but not of" in this way: "not of, but _______ ___________."

- Read Colossians 4:3–6. Describe what the world would experience from our conversations if they were always full of grace and seasoned with salt.

- Journal about a time when you engaged *wholly* with the world while still living *holy* among them.

- With which description in Ken Snell's "castle-dwellers" can you most relate? The castle-dwellers; the missionaries; the "ills" on the outside; the poor, the needy, and oppressed; or the king who lives and suffers outside the walls?

LOVE ALWAYS PROTECTS

As we consider the conditions of the Love-First creed, Paul is not yet done with us in 1 Corinthians 13. Now he gives us the "always" conditions of love.

Love always protects, always trusts, always hopes, always perseveres.

How do we understand these final conditions of divine love? The four words Paul uses as descriptors are not more important than the one word he repeats four times. Paul is pressing the Corinthians and us to develop a culture of love. Yes, protecting, trusting, hoping, and persevering are all characteristics of Christ-conditioned love. But Paul drives home his primary point through the repeated use of *always*. Paul is not advocating occasional good behavior. The Corinthians he writes to are already willing to use good or bad behavior for their own advantage. And this is his point in verses

1–3: even if we have the most sacrificial behavior possible, if it is not rooted in love, it is a mere charade. Paul is calling for a culture of Christ-conditioned love that is always characterized by the qualities he has articulated.

As we contemplate these four conditions of love, whisper to yourself, "*always* . . . this is about *always* . . . this is our *always* culture."

What It Means to Protect

This is a stunning word to launch the "always" section of the love conditions. Paul's word for *protects* is literally the word for *roof*, and the idea is that Christ-conditioned love compels us to always bear whatever we must to cover another person with protection. In 1 Peter 4:8, that apostle uses the same Greek word for "always," but the word in "love each other *deeply*" literally means "continuously." The covering referred to by Peter (in "love covers a multitude of sins") is the word for bark (on a tree), or skin, or a wrap. Our Christ-conditioned culture wraps others in security, love, acceptance, and kindness. This divine mandate was first modeled by Jesus. The Scriptures tell us, "Because God's children are human beings—made of flesh and blood—the *Son also became flesh and blood*" (Heb. 2:14a NLT, emphasis mine). Jesus wrapped himself in our skin—our human experience—so that he can help us. Jesus didn't "visit" humanity on a guest visa. He became a citizen of our state—our human state of being—and then lived as we do. He did not give himself a way to bail out when being among us bruised his reputation. Instead, he chose to associate with tax collectors and sinners—the outcasts of his day.

It has been my experience that Christians are sharply divided over this condition of cultural Christianity. Jesus calls for us to follow him, to love as he did. This means we must investigate his kind of love. So he says, I wrapped my life around you, sin and all, so tightly that it was like your sin showed through my skin. People would actually judge me by your sin. But I loved you too much to have it any other way, even if it meant being convicted, found guilty, and suffering the death penalty for the sins you committed. In Romans 5:6–11, Paul points out to the Roman believers the conditions of God's love. Even when we are powerless, ungodly, sinners, and enemies, he will not abandon the conditions of divine love. That is because God is love. It is not an occasional behavior; it is an identifying mark of the heavenly culture that his reign brings to earth. Then, later in his writing to Titus, Paul punches this point home: "At one time we too were foolish, disobedient, deceived and enslaved by all kinds of passions and pleasures. We lived in malice and envy, being hated and hating one another. *But when the kindness and love of God our Savior appeared, he saved us, not because of righteous things we had done, but because of his mercy*" (3:3–5a, emphasis mine).

Humanity is hater's hell until the kindness and love of God breaks in. But see this for what it is: this is the *real* culture war—the Christ-conditioned culture of love versus the counterfeit culture the Corinthians had concocted. The unconditioned culture of the Corinthian church looked suspiciously like the world, and sometimes worse. Their operating system had been hacked by the virus of envy, pride, and selfish ambition. Not only were they not always covering each other with the protection of love, they were actually suing, cheating, and mistreating each other. Like the recipients of Jude's rebuke, the Corinthians had even brought hate to the Love Feast. How does this happen?

Always Means Always

I believe the answer is not in Paul's words *cover*, *protect*, or *bear*; rather, it is the word *always*. We have been called to a lifestyle, not to an interesting option. As we noted in the beginning of this study, the greatest crisis of our time is not the culture of the world, but the lack of the Christ-conditioned culture in the church. When we think of the Love-First creed as an option, we can see how we are different from the world. Listen again to the words of Jesus:

> If you love those who love you, what credit is that to you? Even sinners love those who love them. And if you do good to those who are good to you, what credit is that to you? Even sinners do that. And if you lend to those from whom you expect repayment, what credit is that to you? Even sinners lend to sinners, expecting to be repaid in full. But love your enemies, do good to them, and lend to them without expecting to get anything back. Then your reward will be great, and you will be children of the Most High, because he is kind to the ungrateful and wicked. (Luke 6:32–35)

My dad warned me about what he called "false finish lines." He wanted to instill in me that there are standards, deadlines, and requirements to every task, job, or calling, and quite often we are ready to quit before the job is done. Frustration, laziness, weariness, and a host of other challenges will tempt us to compromise and settle for a false finish line.

One afternoon Dad sent me to pick up some manhole covers our guys would need for the job the next morning. The traffic was horrible. I missed the exit. It took me miles to get turned around, and the minutes seemed like hours. When I got to the supply company, the gate was locked. Because I missed the exit, I also missed closing time.

I got out of the company truck, climbed up the chain-link fence, and yelled out to the forklift driver. "Please help me. I need the manhole covers."

"We are closed," he replied.

I wanted to yell, "No kidding, Sherlock, that's why I'm clinging to a chain-link fence yelling for you!" But I kept that to myself and pleaded with him. He finally opened the gate and loaded my truck.

I got back into traffic and made it to the job site. My dad's employees would arrive the next morning and have what they needed.

I made it home, but it was late—well after dark. I plopped down in a chair at our kitchen table where Dad was reading his newspaper, and I let out a sigh. I was bushed. As I was about to put a spoonful of mashed potatoes in my mouth, he said, "Good job tonight." My dad had already called over to the supply company to make sure I had the load. I said, "Thanks."

That might not sound like much to you, but it meant the world to me, and still does. With his simple choice of words, he was acknowledging something very important: I was understanding the culture of business—no false finish lines.

Covering each other, protecting each other, giving the kind of Christ-conditioned love that sinners need can be hard, frustrating, painful. But this is the way of Christ, and it is the condition of his Love-First creed.

Some Christians have the reputation of being brittle and frail. The slightest provocation throws them. This may be because they do not believe in the *always* condition of divine love. They believe they are called to give protection and cover to others, but only when they want to, and only to people they are related to, want to impress, want to get something from, or are afraid of. In the end, this is not love. But if they do not like someone, feel insecure, are seeking revenge, hope to bring them down a notch, or are easily angered, then they abandon the call to *always* protect.

Christians use the "righteous indignation" excuse to escape the *always* condition. They imagine that their superiority in holiness makes them the exception to the *always* clause. But this is not an either/or condition. *Always* means always. So even if—no, especially when—someone offends you, this is the real test of your *always* love. Will you accept a false finish line, or will you abide by the *always* condition. Manhole covers have an awful lot of you-know-what underneath, so maybe they are a good metaphor for the love that covers a multitude of sins. It doesn't mean that we ignore sin, enjoy sin, or scoff at the consequences of sin. But it does mean that no sinner ever—*ever*—should have to wonder if they are loved.

People will often object, "But aren't we supposed to be angry at sin?" Yes, that is one of the appropriate responses to sin. But here are two essential steps to help you catch yourself before you sidestep a Christ-condition of divine love to suit your own selfish self:

- Be most angry at your own sin. Channel your greatest fervor against your own failings. Highlight your own hypocrisy with the brightest light. Confess only your own sins. Be the most public and detailed about your own sin. Never dig up more details on someone else's sin than you will publicly divulge about your own sin.
- When it is necessary to point out the sin that may be ravaging someone else's life, do not get involved unless you are willing to suffer with them. Jesus suffers with us. He stands with us. He does not maintain a safe distance. The deepest declaration of love is the "I am with you always" promise of Jesus. When he promises, "I will never leave you nor forsake you," this includes being faithful when we are not. When was the last time you fought through your frustration with someone else to be faithful to them when it challenged every fiber of your being?

Always stand up for sinners when they come up in conversation. If you are in a small group and someone starts talking about—railing about—someone else's sin, run to the side of the accused and stand with the condemned. You will find Jesus there.

Love-First Reflections

- The Greek word for "protect" is also the word for roof. How does the word roof help us with our understanding for this condition of Christ's love?
- In what way did Jesus wrap his life around ours? What were the consequences of this kind of love?
- What are the essential steps to making sure your love always protects?
- If you always stand up for sinners when they come up in conversation, and you run to the accused to stand with the condemned, who will you find there?

LOVE ALWAYS TRUSTS

Love always trusts that something can be more than what is.

Do you have a favorite Jesus story? His insight into the human condition is unmatched. He has the uncanny capacity to catch us off guard, in a good way, to open windows of understanding.

Jesus tells a story about workmen who believed they got cheated on their pay because the farmer who hired them didn't pay them more than he promised (Matt. 20:1–16). They accused the landowner of being inequitable, not trustworthy. Jesus allows us to step into their sandals and feel the apparent inequity. The story sets us up. We smell our own sweat and parched throats. We feel the growing anticipation that fairness demands an outcome other than what was promised.

Then Jesus asks three questions, each more difficult than the previous:

- Didn't you agree to these wages?

- Don't I have the right to do what I want with my own money?
- Are you envious because I am generous?

Jesus moves them to see that they were the ones "cheating" on the terms of payment. Not content to just challenge behavior, Jesus presses them to see that the heart that cannot be trusted is their own, due to envy. In his list of the conditions of love, Paul writes that love does not envy, but love always trusts. Had love (and not envy) been the driving force behind their assessment of the farmer, the workers would have had no lack of trust in him.

In Jesus's stories, prostitutes, foreigners, and tax collectors are the heroes. They are the ones who help the downtrodden, have humble and grateful hearts, and show the most promise for faithfulness and generosity. He trusts them with the gospel message, with community benevolence, and with a chance to be shining examples for the new humanity he is proclaiming. Zacchaeus is on the front page of Jesus's discipleship journal on the first day of his new life. He is Exhibit A for the marvelous truth that, with Jesus, trustworthiness is about the direction you are headed, not about the distance you've traveled. Yes, it is wise to give people the opportunity to "prove" themselves in a given competency, but time and track record are not an assurance of trustworthiness.

I had a person tell me that "past behavior is the best indicator of future behavior." On the surface, this sounded kind of right. Why would I put it that way? It makes total sense to my mind, but it seems to compete with Jesus's capacity to redeem and convert. As I began to research this statement, I found that psychologists, behavioral scientists, and business analysts do not agree. After reading several articles, blogs, and research documents, I came to the realization that this is an oversimplified mantra that has been around for decades but has gained the most traction with the rise of pop-psychology. Hard research bears out that this maxim is true only if a myriad of other factors are taken into account, and it does not play out in a larger consideration of data points.[1]

It turns out that like most things in life, this mantra is useful only when it is applied reservedly and not as a categorical judgment. This is the case in point with

- The woman at the well (John 4)
- Matthew and Zacchaeus (Luke 19)
- The woman caught in adultery (John 8)
- The Prodigal Son (Luke 15)
- Saul, who became the apostle Paul (Acts 9)
- John Mark the deserter, who became John Mark the faithful servant (Acts 15; 2 Tim. 4)
- John the Son of Thunder, who became John the Apostle of Love (Luke 9)
- Peter the denier, who became Peter the witness (Luke 22)

This is the story of Jesus, and it pervades the love of his disciples. Notice that the writer of Hebrews, after he drops the hammer on their immaturity and drifting faithfulness, assures his readers, "Even though we speak like this, dear friends, we are convinced of better things in your case" (6:9a).

The story of God is a story of love that always trusts. But how do we understand this condition of love over and against the litany of scriptures warning us to be prudent, discerning, and wise as serpents? Even Jesus did not entrust himself to everyone (John 2:24–25). He knew that others were not to be trusted with his own integrity or ministry. He would not hold others accountable to be the resources or motivation for who he would be or for what he came to do. That he did not entrust himself does not mean he did not trust what was possible for them. Jesus lived by the default of love, and this meant that he communicated to others that the life they had lived up to the point of meeting him was not the only life possible for them. I know countless marriages that have overcome an affair, never to repeat the unfaithfulness again. Our church is filled with courageous people who used to be all things unholy before Jesus became Savior and King in their lives.

One Sunday morning a deacon from our church approached me. He mentioned that some people from Oregon who had known me when I was a "hoodlum" were visiting our church and wanted to say hello. Great! Another encounter with my past. Another torturing walk down the dark alley of memory.

Some months later, a similar situation unfolded, but this time it was a teacher of mine from high school. "Great, here we go again," I thought. But it was delightful. She and her husband were so kind, generous, and loving. For a while I thought she must have been suffering from memory loss, or maybe she had me mixed up with someone else. But then she brought me back to reality. She said to the small group of interested parishioners who had gathered around, "Well, I always thought Donny would either become a preacher or go to prison." Everyone laughed, and so did I, this time. The twinkle in her eye and the warmth of her tone signaled something different about her. She seemed genuinely pleased that I wasn't in prison! I thanked her for being so kind and encouraging. She then shared, "I decided a long time ago to remember all my students with grace." Paul has already reminded us that "love keeps no record of wrongs," and this is an essential condition for the culture of always trusting.

Love's culture of trust suggests that the church creates a culture in which people are inspired to live up to the higher ideals possible for them. A false superiority goes with a culture of condescension. Jesus tells about two men going to the temple to pray, one a religious leader and the other a despised tax collector. By now we ought to have our eyes and ears wide open to the way Jesus will flip a narrative on its head, but this one still catches us by surprise:

> To some who were confident of their own righteousness and looked down on everyone else, Jesus told this parable: "Two men went up to the temple to pray, one a Pharisee and the other a tax collector. The Pharisee stood by himself and prayed: 'God, I thank you that I am not like other people—robbers, evildoers, adulterers—or even like this tax collector. I fast twice a week and give a tenth of all I get.'
>
> "But the tax collector stood at a distance. He would not even look up to heaven, but beat his breast and said, 'God, have mercy on me, a sinner.'
>
> "I tell you that this man, rather than the other, went home justified before God. For all those who exalt themselves will be humbled, and those who humble themselves will be exalted." (Luke 18:9–14)

The problem is spelled out clearly: exalting ourselves, even under the guise of having advanced integrity, spirituality, and holiness, will end in our spiritual demise. Better to level the playing field on our own than for God to have to knock us off our pedestal. But how? Paul says it comes through Christ-conditioned love. The person who loves as Christ does always believes more about what God can do in someone than what that person has done with themselves.

When the apostle Paul was a new follower of Jesus, the Christians did not trust him. His past was their predictor of the future. Even the brother called directly by God to share the gospel with Paul did not want to because of Paul's past. But there was a man, a lover of God and lover of people, whom God knew he could count on. We find this story in Acts 9:26–28. Barnabas showed great trust in God by being willing to take the Christian-killer Paul under his wing and stand up for him. This had a meaningful effect on the church, but an everlasting effect on Paul. Barnabas continued to include Paul in church-related activities that demonstrated his trust in Paul. Will you get burned when you trust others? Well, let's see . . . Yahweh was, Jesus was, the Spirit was, and Jesus said you would be. So I think that is a *yes*. I'm not trying to make light of the pain any of us have experienced. I'm using this tone with myself as much as anyone else to remind us that too often our expectations of love have not been conditioned by the explicit teachings of Christ.

Let's face it. The teachings of Jesus on this belong in the "I can't do this anymore" category. He taught his disciples to love their enemies, do good, and bless "those who mistreat you" (Luke 6:27–28). "Mistreat you" is not taking the last glazed donut or forgetting your birthday. In the original text this word means to hurt, insult, despitefully use, wrongfully accuse. There is no escaping the weight of this word. So how in the world can love always trust when others can break our hearts?

The trust Paul is advocating is not transactional trust of personal relationships, the reciprocation of truth-telling and truth-receiving. Paul is calling for a redemptive approach to humanity's potential, the belief that people can be raised to a new life. This is Paul's core message to the Corinthians: protect means trusting love when it seems like love won't work. It means trusting love when we want to reach for condemnation, hate, or ambivalence.

Always trusting means not quitting on love when it feels like love has quit on you. Always trusting means being love to others when they have not been love to you.

Love-First Reflections

- Why is trustworthiness more about the *direction* you are headed than the *distance* you've traveled?

- Choose from the eight examples given below. Read the text and reflect on how God "trusted" them. How did His trust change their lives? Now, write in first person *how the trust Jesus placed in you is changing your life.*

  The woman at the well (John 4:1–42)
  Zacchaeus (Luke 19:1–10)
  The woman caught in adultery (John 8:1–11)
  The Prodigal Son (Luke 15:11–32)
  Saul who became Paul (Acts 9: -30)
  John Mark (Acts 15:3–40; 2 Timothy 4:11)
  John, the Son of Thunder (Luke 9:51–56; 1 John 4:16–17)
  Peter (Luke 22:54–62; Acts 2:14–41)

- What are the benefits that come from believing more in what God can do in a person's life than what they can do on their own?

- Fill in the blank. "Always trusting means not _______________ on love when it feels love has _________on you. Always trusting means being love to _______________ when they have not been love to __________."

20

LOVE NEVER GIVES UP

When I was eleven, I stole a bicycle chain and lock from a department store. I didn't want anyone to steal my bike. (Once again, this book enhances your compassion for my parents.) After I successfully shoplifted the lock and chain, I became a regular. Soon, I had quite a store of stolen goods under my mattress.

I couldn't sleep, and it wasn't because of the lump of pilfered treasure I was sleeping on. My fifth-grade mind was wracked with guilt, and I was a wreck. I walked past my dad three or four times, pausing long enough for him to look up and say, "What's up?" "Nothing," I would choke out, and then go back to my room. What was I going to do? Finally I went up to him, burst into tears, and couldn't get anything to come out of my mouth. I just motioned to him to follow me. We went into my bedroom, where I threw up the mattress to expose the evidence of my transgressions.

He looked a little puzzled. What in the world? A can of paint, some dice, a blacklight poster, the chain and lock, and a smashed vinyl record. I know . . . give me a break. I was eleven! In between my heaving sobs I told him the sordid story of my crime spree. We finally sat down on the bedroom floor and came up with a plan. I earned money from selling newspapers, and I had enough to pay for the stolen goods. (Crime does not always make sense!) The plan was for me to return the goods, *and* pay for them, and take whatever punishment the infractions deserved.

When Dad and I arrived at the store, I was carrying the bag of loot. We found the manager. I was fighting back the tears as I handed him the strange bag of items and explained what I had done. Then I gave him the money to pay for them. I guess it was my lucky day, because the store manager decided to make an example of me in front of a growing crowd of bobbing heads and stares. He loudly scolded me for my misdeeds, and I hung my head. I said I was sorry. I felt so awful. But he just kept going. I guess he didn't get many repentant shoplifters to yell at, so maybe I was taking one for the team. But it started to get a little extreme. He began to lay into me about what a sorry son I was and that he was sure my parents had to be so ashamed of me.

That final statement evoked a different voice, one that would meet me in my messes and move me toward the light many times over. Dad gently interrupted the store manager, twenty years his junior, and asked, "Have you said your piece?" The store manager took a much-needed breath (I needed him to take that breath!).

"What?" he stammered.

"Have you said your piece?" my dad repeated. "Are you satisfied with the consequences?"

"Well, yes. I guess so," he reluctantly acquiesced.

"Then," my dad continued, "how about if *you* be the store manager, and *I* will be his dad?"

And with that, we walked out of the store. "And I will be his dad . . ." meant that I was still his son.

This was not a moment with him; it was a way of life. Throughout my young life he would stand by me many times when my shame splashed over onto him. He wouldn't pay my fines or court costs, but he paid the price of love, always trusting that somewhere along the path a better me would emerge. Eight years later while he was standing in a courtroom by my side, my heart finally broke. My rebellious self was drowning in the sea of Christ-conditioned love. The judge looked at me, but said to my dad, "I'm sorry, Mr. McLaughlin, that you had to be saddled with a son like this." I thought to myself, "He's right. Dad has no business even being seen with me, let alone standing by me." The judge ordered my fine and penalty. I went by the pay window while dad waited by the door. We walked out in the Portland rain together and then stepped into an Italian restaurant close by. We shook off the cold, sat down in a booth, and I stared at the table. He said, "I heard what the judge said, but I want you to hear what I have to say. I've always loved you. I love you today. And I will always love you." I know in my heart that I have been a different person from that day forward. I can track the trajectory of my life from that declaration of love that finally got through to me.

Lessons Learned Become Lessons Applied

We made a declaration at our church two decades ago that we would not remember people for their lowest moments. But we found it easier to condition our love with trust when the people we were forgiving or encouraging were people we liked. Yes, *people we liked.*

Let me bring you inside on this one. We began to notice a disparity between the way we reacted to people who fit into our categorical "nice and naughty" lists. Part of the confusion was that for different people, the same category may end up on one person's like-list and another person's disgust-list. Now what follows here is going to sound really petty, and it is, but sometimes we just have to get down to the ugly truth. Here is what we saw . . .

- Political Parties—We were guilty of judging candidates by their party affiliation, but worse, we judged brothers and sisters in Christ along the same party lines. I know that sounds absurd, but we did, and it gets worse.
- Collegiate Sports—Now this one may be more of an SEC-centric sin, but I don't really think so. It's one thing to have rivalries, but I began to hear fans describe their programs and players with terms of righteousness and traditional values! I am smiling right now as I keyboard this, because it is just nuts. You may think we must be hapless and hopeless, but look around. You may find the same problems right where you are. (Warning: It gets worse!)
- Churches—We were guilty of judging and fault-finding with other Christians. Whatever the Baptists, Methodists, Presbyterians, and whatever other one-named community church were doing to thrive among us, we were quick to dismiss them with tones of great concern about their error. If they had a lively worship, we would make judgments about entertainment. If they had a doctrinal difference with us, there was no way we were off . . . oh, no way possible. And, of course, we could critique ourselves, but stunningly we would find no glaring faults or doctrinal fallacies. It was quite amazing how orthodox we were in our own eyes while we were giving no heart at all to the "love always trusts" condition laid down in Scripture. *Just going* to one of "those other" churches made you suspect. By our own muscle and a shovel we buried other believers alive.
- Disgusting Christians—I've heard it said that Christians are the only army that shoots their own wounded, but now I've seen the carnage up close. It turned out that we had categories of sinners. Some were worth running into the field of battle to rescue, and others were turned

> on as enemies themselves. Some we believed in, others were simply disgusting. Some worth saving. Some worth stoning.

Slowly grace and truth began to flush us out. We were duplicitous. We were dishonest. We would express love toward a family in our church while railing against the very people they loved. We were two-faced, and God exposed it. We would act loving when it suited us and then be disgracefully demeaning toward those who disgusted us when we thought everyone around the table agreed. And worse, we would come up with justification for those we liked.

We were an unholy, unloving, unconditioned mess.

But the gnawing grind of grace kept working on us. Jesus loved us so well that it became harder and harder to not love each other. He expressed eternal commitment to our potential to live up to his glorious vision for us, though we were so far from being what he called us to be. How could we choke the life out of a fallen or failing sibling of the Savior when that very Savior was cheering us on? The hypocrisy turned to humility, and we fell on our knees before the One who loved us first.

The Love-First creed of divinely conditioned love seemed to be the only possible option for a people loved so well by God. He never gives up on the potential of us all, so how could we do anything other than that? Through Christ, we can do all things, and this is where we find the sustaining strength to never give up.

Love-First Reflections

- Journal about someone in your life who didn't give up on you when you were close to giving up on yourself.

- Have you ever discovered that some sins are easier to forgive than others? Are there some sins that are too offensive for even the blood of Christ to cover?

- How can "coming clean" about treating some "sinners" with more grace and respect than others bring us to our knees before the One who first loved us?

- When we never give up on others, we are a living witness of the love of God. How can we examine our motives to make sure our commitment to others is truly motivated by God's love in us?

LOVE ALWAYS HOPES

Every time I think he has hit rock bottom,
he proves there's lower still.

Twenty years ago, our church responded to a challenge to dive deeper into ministries that expressed the matchless love of God to people in addiction and recovery. We were already hosting some Alcoholics Anonymous groups, providing a room, some cookies, and a facilitator. This kept us close enough to claim success when people stayed sober and distant enough to shield us from the real pain of addiction and recovery.

But God used a middle-school teacher with a furious passion to help others change all this. Soon our church was host to over one hundred recovering addicts every Sunday, with a growing number of "alumni" who would slip back into addiction, only to reenter recovery, and recommit to our church family. This ministry became a definining part of the reputation of our church in the community, with over four hundred attending our weekly support groups.

This might sound like a dream come true from your perspective on Christ, the church, and our mission in the world, but it was not so easy. Imagine a predominantly middle- and upper-middle-class suburban church suddenly deluged with a flood of refugees from the world of addiction. Most of us could not have identified cocaine if it had been on a plate and labeled. We had been hosting AA groups for years, so how tough could this be . . . right?

Can I just admit that as a church we often felt like one of those viral videos where some toothless guy in a ball cap yells, "Hey, y'all, watch this!" right before he crashes his V-8-powered lawn tractor into the side of a barn! We've had plenty of bumps along the road, and these included:

- The church soundboard was stolen to purchase illegal drugs. The replacement for the stolen one was stolen before we even unpacked it from the box. The third one was chained to the sound booth.
- The church van was stolen. One of our brothers relapsed and took it on a two-week tour up I-95 selling cocaine out of the sliding door on which the church name was painted in bold letters! That had to be just about the perfect cover for a drug dealer.
- Sometimes a few colorful cuss words got mixed in when folks were sharing their testimonies.
- One of our ladies at church had her purse stolen right off the pew.

Yes. Did I mention we had no idea what would happen if we would say yes to Jesus's leadership? You may have noticed, the word "yes" played a significant role in the forward movement of these events. That is because love always hopes. Love always looks and longs for the redemption of God to show itself in the lives of people, no matter how hopeless the starting point appears. And there were plenty of challenges.

But perhaps the greatest challenge Jesus had in this process was getting us to see that the ministry to addicts was here to change *us*. We needed to minister to them so that they could transform us. We are all in recovery from something, but we didn't know it. We learned from courageous spiritual warriors battling addiction what it meant to never lose hope. We learned that it is easier to quote scriptures about hope than to maintain hope *always*.

We needed to minister to them so that they could transform us. We are all in recovery from something, but we didn't know it.

The key to this transformation unfolding among us is love. Love always hopes. It is love that gives energy to hope. When we love someone like God has loved us, hope is birthed in the relationship. Dallas Willard speaks to the power of God's love:

> Injury brings pain and loss, then fear and anger, which mingle with resentment and contempt and settle into postures of coldness and malice, with brutal feelings that drain the body of health and strength and shatter the social well-being. In such a world God intrudes, gently and in many ways, but especially in the person of Jesus Christ. It is he who stands for love, as no one else has ever done, and pays the price for it. His crucifixion is the all-time high-water mark of love on earth. No other source, whether inside or outside religions, even comes close to what God in Christ shows of love. This is the first "move" of love in the process of redemption. "He first loved us" (1 John 4:19). Therefore, "Love is from God," and, "We know love by this, that He laid down His life for us." All other loves are to be measured by

> this standard. Love is awakened in us by him. We feel its call. "We love because He first loved us."[1]

As we waded into the pain of addiction recovery with our brothers and sisters, we discovered that each of us had our own pain to deal with. Working so closely with people in recovery held up the mirror of self-examination to the rest of our church. We might not use cocaine, but we still exhibit negative behavior associated with our internal frustration and personal sin. Most Christians do not feel comfortable sharing their darkest thoughts and actions, but this leaves us buried in frustrations and hopelessness. Our unconfessed sin and unconscious hopelessness weakened our capacity to love others without losing hope for them.

A brother called me on the phone and asked if we could have lunch. Now well into retirement, he had experienced a close call with his health. Eternity was looming as never before, and he was in need of some closure. After the appetizer arrived at our table, he started his story thirty years earlier when he had come to his senses and turned his life over to the Lord. In the years following his acceptance of Christ, he married a beautiful lady, and they had shared every step of their spiritual journey. But I noticed he had an uncharitable side to him. He could be hypercritical and make raw, unfounded snap judgments.

He looked me square in the eyes and asked, "Am I just wasting my time?" I was somewhat surprised and replied, "About what?" "My Christian life . . . going to heaven . . . being saved. Am I probably going to hell anyway?"

"Whoa, whoa, whoa," I thought as I was getting my bearings. "Why are you thinking this way?" I asked.

His words came in a sluggish crawl, "Jeanie isn't my first wife."

"Okay," I thought, "this is about him wondering if he is living in sin and cannot be forgiven." So I asked him, "Are you afraid that God cannot forgive you and redeem you from your past life of sin?"

With a bit of an anxious, louder tone he asked, "Do you think he can?"

I replied, "I sure hope so."

At the end of the day, all our hope is rooted in the love God has for us. Our sin causes injury and pain, but not just to others. It can kill our hope. But the story of the love of God is a restorer of hope. Hope arrived in every home Jesus entered and in every heart that opened wide to him. It is Jesus who inspired the apostle Paul to write:

> Since we have been justified through faith, we have peace with God through our Lord Jesus Christ, through whom we have gained access by faith into this grace in which we now stand. And we boast in the hope of the glory of God. Not only so, but we also glory in our sufferings, because we know that suffering produces perseverance; perseverance, character; and character, hope. And hope does not put us to shame, because God's love has been poured out into our hearts through the Holy Spirit, who has been given to us. (Rom. 5:1–5)

Just as it is true that "hurt people hurt people," so it is equally true that hope-filled people fill others with hope. That does not mean that hope is easy to maintain. Desmond Tutu, purveyor of hope under the most difficult of circumstances, shared, "Hope is being able to see that there is light despite all of the darkness." In fact, the apostle Paul notes that when you can see *how* things are going to work out, or *that* things will get better, that is no hope at all: "Hope that is seen is no hope at all. Who hopes for what they already have?" But if we Christians "hope for what we do not yet have," Paul says, "we wait for it patiently" (Rom. 8:24–25).

The Hebrews writer shares this powerful inspiration, "Now faith is confidence in what we hope for and assurance about what we do not see" (11:1), but then this famous chapter is filled with stories where people had to follow the Lord when it would seem all hope was lost. Paul picks up on this same theme as he considers the righteous walk of Abraham. The descriptions of Abraham and Sarah in both Romans 4 and Hebrews 11 are virtually comical. I promise you they would have watched their language about Sarah a little more carefully had she been standing right there. But listen to the testimony of hope: "Against all hope, Abraham in hope believed and so became the father of many nations, just as it had been said to him . . ." (Rom. 4:18). "Against all hope . . . In hope . . ." This theme was central to the sustaining strength of civil rights leader, Martin Luther King Jr. He said, "We must accept finite disappointment, but *never lose infinite hope*."

The divinely conditioned love of Christ, rooted in the love of God the Father, never gives in to the hopelessness of momentary losses. Jesus's insistence on bringing hope to the nations was a thorn in the side of the religious elite in his day because he often interrupted their Sabbath services to bring hope to the hurting. There are at least seven of these "Sabbath healings" among the miracles of Jesus. What is most fascinating is the callousness of the religious leaders toward their parishioners who were hurting. One woman had not been able to stand up for eighteen years. Jesus called her forward for healing (Luke 13:10–17). When Jesus set her free, she immediately praised God. What more could her spiritual leader want, right? Wrong! He's a killjoy during the healed woman's happy dance because Jesus set her free on the wrong day!

This is the sad story of religion: the loveless creeds supersede the need for love. When love's light grows dim, the flicker of hope goes out. Religion suggests that God is unconcerned with our hurts and hopes, and it judges mostly by what we say and do in regard to doctrine and the practice of religious rituals. This is simply not valid. Churches that major in hope are lighthouses of the unfailing love of God that always hopes.

When he heals the lame man on the Sabbath in John 5, Jesus is severely criticized. They are not buying Jesus's claim that "the Sabbath was made for man, not man for the Sabbath." So Jesus drops a bombshell on them that also goes over poorly, "My Father is always at his work to this very day, and I too am working." Jesus lets them in on a little secret about God's work schedule. God can work, and is working, always. Whenever God is at work, there is always hope!

Churches that major in hope will thrive. Churches that minor in hope writhe. I've been in both. The Love-First creed exposes people to divine love. It rekindles their spiritual fires by restoring their hope. If God can reach them where they are, how much more is possible, and not just for them, but for all the broken.

When Jesus heals the Gerasene man who had been possessed by a legion of demons, the man wants immediately to join Jesus in telling others. But he is not alone. Person after person redeemed from their awful pit become "carriers" infected with a highly contagious hope.

But there are those who are against hope, or at least against the "always" kind of hope in the Christ-creed. Too much hope means too much grace, and too much grace means too much reliance on God's control instead of their own. This is most powerfully illustrated in the story of the Prodigal Father. You know the story of the extravagant father who appears to waste the riches of his love hoping for the return of his lost and wayward son. Upon the younger brother's return, the older brother's worst fears are confirmed: the father's love is unbounded, unconditional. The angry brother's resentment-fueled outburst at his father rages about the waste and excess on this sibling the older brother had written off long ago, assigning him to the "hopeless" column. But now it is the father who is hopeless—hopelessly foolish and frivolous.

Can you not relate at least somewhat to the older brother? Doesn't the application of God's grace seem out of bounds sometimes?

But let's quickly return to the story. Is the father's love for his sons actually *un*conditioned? No! In fact it is the exact opposite. Notice the father's response to his older son, "We had to celebrate." "It is necessary" to celebrate. The father tells the older brother what is necessary, what is essential. We had to celebrate "hope realized" when your brother returned. The older brother can seem somewhat pathetic, if not villainous, in this passage, but who can't relate to him? Who doesn't struggle with whether or not we are being too loose with grace?

Clues to what is happening with this older brother are given in the first ten verses of the chapter (Luke 15). Jesus is surrounded by tax collectors, thugs, and sinners—outsiders who are not used to being insiders—and religious leaders who are insiders caught on the outside, and this seating chart is not working for them. But why? Wouldn't religious leaders want the "sinners" to get a little religion? Perhaps the greater sin of Jesus was giving these tax collectors and their minions false hope. Surely they were too far gone to repent. I guess it might be easier to have such a hopeless opinion of someone whom your religious rules forbid you to even eat with. The creed of the Pharisees was rooted in separatism, and they thought it was proof of their holiness, their commitment to the truth. The way is narrow, so the more separate, the more holy, right? So, as they were grumbling about Jesus accepting these no-goods, he told them two stories. One was about a sheep lost far away, but the second about a coin lost right at home. Two lost items: one far away, one right at home. Now notice Luke 15:11: "Jesus continued: there was a man who had two sons . . ."

The story of the sheep and the coin are not really about animals and money at all: these are stories about two lost boys—one lost far away and one lost right in his own home. The tax collectors know they are lost, and Jesus gives them a glimmer of hope that their religion withholds from them. But the Pharisees, like the older brother, are lost at home and do not see it. They are selfish, brutally insensitive to the heart of the Father and the plight of his children. They can only judge. They peddle a false holiness where all the necessary components provide a neat little package of do's and don'ts that will hopefully put God in their debt come Judgment Day. But this loveless religiosity is exposed when the undeserving, who along with hope they had cast aside, are welcomed into the heavenly Kingdom with a celebration orchestrated by none other than God himself. The Prodigal Father is the Prodigal God . . . the One who never gives up on his children.

Replacing Hurt with Hope

I waited for David in the church parking lot while we finished our conversation on the phone. We hung up our phones, and he stumbled toward me and gave me a tired, "Hey, what's up?" That's a guy's way of saying, "Thanks for meeting up to talk."

Now we sit across from each other in my office. His shirt is damp from sweat. His eyes red and weary. He repeats most of our phone conversation, talking to me but trying to make sense for himself. So I ask, "When you saw the text from Jerry on Kim's phone, what happened next?"

David regurgitates the story. "She grabbed her phone and tried to delete it. We argued. She lied. I asked if there were more . . . you know . . . texts, emails, pics. She nodded, slumped over at the kitchen table, and pushed her phone toward me. I started reading. I felt dizzy. Light-headed. I asked her, 'Do you love him?' She was crying, 'I don't know. It's so confusing.'"

Honesty. Devastating honesty.

David continues, "I was sick at my stomach. I wanted to run. My world was crumbling, and I headed for the door. But she, now standing between me and the door, grasped my hand and cried,

'Don't leave. Please don't. *I need your help.*' So I stopped, held her hand, and stared at the floor."

My heart was aching for David, and for Kim. How do things get like this? The creep of complacency, the slow death of devotion, the intrigue of feeling interesting again? Did love just up and die but we missed the funeral? When later I met with Kim, I asked, "Do you love David?"

She replied, "I think so. I mean, yes . . . of course . . . I don't know . . . if I ever have."

David faced the same question. He later reflected, "I guess I always thought I loved Kim, but the moment I knew it was when she said, 'I need your help.' My heart was a mess and my mind was a wreck, but when she asked for help, I couldn't walk away."

The Story of God's Love

You may find it surprising, that God's love story reads somewhat like David and Kim's. There are many chapters in the story, so I do not want to oversimplify, but let your imagination wrap itself around the parent-child metaphor found in Hosea 11. God our Father says, "When Israel was a child, I loved him, and I called my son out of Egypt. But the more I called to him, the farther he moved from me, offering sacrifices to the images of Baal and burning incense to idols." Then Hosea expands imagery in terms that will capture any parent's heart. The Father recalls, "I myself taught Israel how to walk, leading him along by the hand. But he doesn't know or even care that it was I who took care of him. . . . I myself stooped to feed him, but my people are determined to desert me. They call me the Most High, but they don't truly honor me."

Because his much-loved child has turned his back on him, the Father resolves to allow ruin to come crashing down. But then, like any loving parent, God has second thoughts about such punishment. "Oh, how can I give you up, Israel?" he wails. "How can I let you go? How can I destroy you? . . . My heart is torn within me, and my compassion overflows." Then God explains his hesitance to let Israel suffer for their sins. The grieving Father refuses to give up on his son. "No, I will not unleash my fierce anger. I will not completely destroy Israel, for I am God and not a mere mortal. I am the Holy One living among you, and I will not come to destroy." Why? Because the Father's hope is not gone. "Someday the people will follow me. . . . And I will bring them home again" (11:1–11 NLT).

It's hard not to notice that God's love sounds so much like our own experience. When David and I shared this passage in my office, he started to cry. "It's so weird to see God in my shoes," he said, "and I'm not trying to disrespect him." I assured David that I believe this is exactly why this passage is in the Bible. We are supposed to see God in our shoes, and us in his. God loves, and is betrayed, and wants to turn away, but his heart is torn, and he can't just flip a switch and shut down love.

God knows all of us need to see how he maintains hope when love hurts. Our souls growl, "I just can't do this anymore." We are tired, and tired of hurting. Our hearts feel hollow, our beds are lonely, and no amount of self-medicating soothes the wound. And yet we cannot turn off love. In a messed-up kind of way, the pain we feel is evidence of the interminable desire to love and be loved. And this is why God doesn't walk out on Israel, or you.

David and Kim are in love now, and they know it. Maybe Dad was right. Maybe the divine love of the Christ-creed isn't fully known until someone gives us a reason not to love.

Love-First Reflections

- "Too much hope means too much grace, and too much grace means too much reliance on God's control rather than their own." Do your best to explain why some might prefer limited hope and limited grace based on a list that they can check off.

- The older brother in the story of the Prodigal Son thought his father was too loose with the grace toward his brother. Have you ever thought that God's extravagant grace may incite extravagant sin?

- Read Luke 15:1–32. In each of the three parables Jesus told, we identify being lost far away with the sheep and the prodigal son and being lost at home with the coin and the older brother. Who were the Pharisees in these parables? Who do you most closely identify with?

- Read Hosea 11:1–10. Why does God hold out hope for his child, Israel?

LOVE ALWAYS ENDURES

Let me remind you of a central premise in this book: *You can't get God right if you get love wrong.*

Yes. I believe every word I just wrote. Church people are famous for loving doctrine while hating each other. Would you like to email me right now and say, "Not our church—we *all* love each other." I was going to give you my email address, but the publisher nixed that idea. So I will just respond and tell you how happy I am that the three of you are enjoying your religious paradise! But for the rest of us, a brief stop in Reformation Europe or in a church business meeting makes my point just fine.

I am not sure if Paul held out this final "always" quality of love as a catch-all, or as the "secret sauce" of divinely conditioned love. This quality is different from patience and the other conditions that encourage the "long view" of love. The Greek word for *endure* means to "remain under." There are all kinds of implications for this aspect of love, but Paul always focuses on the example of Jesus. The Hebrews writer encourages his readers to come alive again to their fellowship with each other and devotion to God, but their vision correction is rediscovered only in Christ. "Let us throw off everything that hinders and the sin that so easily entangles. And let us run with perseverance the race marked out for us, fixing our eyes on Jesus, the pioneer and perfecter of faith," he encourages us. Then he cites Jesus as an example of such vision: "For the joy set before him he endured the cross, scorning its shame, and sat down at the right hand of the throne of God. Consider him who endured such opposition from sinners, so that you will not grow weary and lose heart" (12:1b–3).

Our families, communities, nations, and churches are facing an unprecedented *awareness* of our fractured and frayed relationships. My words are carefully chosen because I do not believe we are more factious and vicious toward each other than ever before. But I do believe social media floods us with gruesome scenes and gory images that sear our souls with horrific violence. Humans can be grotesquely inhumane.

Does it not seem inconceivable that when writing down the essentials of the true Christian faith in order to get our *heads* straight, we failed to see the need to align our *hearts* with Jesus?

It came to me in the research for this book that by the way our ancient creeds were conceived and codified, later adherents could conceivably kill other Christians without being unfaithful to the creed. Love is nowhere to be found in our ancient creeds, and seldom in the way they were devised or defended. But you may argue, "Don't we have Christ's example and instruction about love in the Bible?" My answer is, "Yes, emphatically yes!" But the problem we face is that creeds condensed what the authorities at that time thought was essential to promote pure doctrinal truth and to fend off heresy. And this was a noble work. But does it not seem inconceivable that when writing down the essentials of the true Christian faith in order to get our *heads* straight, we failed to see the need to align our *hearts* with Jesus? The Christian community forgot to apply what Christ said is the *first and greatest* command. What might history have been like if every creed had been prefaced with the conditions of Christ? Let's review our Love-First Creed:

> **I believe** that God is love.
>
> **I believe** that God so loved the world that he gave his only Son so that the world may be saved through him.
>
> **I believe** that God loved me when I was a powerless, ungodly sinner and enemy.
>
> **I believe** that the first and greatest command is to love God with all that I am.
>
> **I believe** that with the first and greatest command, I am to love my neighbor as myself.
>
> **I believe** that I must love my enemies, the ungrateful, and the wicked.
>
> **I believe** that if I claim to love God but do not love others, I am a liar.
>
> **I believe** that when I see my brothers and sisters in need, I must help them with my material possessions, or the love of God is not in me.

To gain a sense for the powerful impact this creed can have on our personal and congregational witness worldwide, read back through each statement and adjust all the personal pronouns to the first-person plural *we*. These eight we-believe statements represent the summation and codification of Christ's orthodoxy. Our willingness to put into practice the Love-First creed of Christ—properly prioritizing his divinely conditioned love as articulated in Scripture—will restore to our faith the community-impacting and globally transforming vision of the gospel. For this vision, love will endure all things.

Love-First Reflections

- Fill in the blanks. "You can't get God __________ if you get love __________."

- The Greek word for "endure" means
  ________________ ____________________.

- Read Hebrews 12:1–3. Jesus "remained under" the suffering of "the cross" and "such opposition from sinners." His love remained; his love endured. Reflect on a situation when someone gave you reason *not to remain* but your love endured even through suffering?

- How might history have been different if the church had codified the first and greatest command in its creeds and confessions of faith?

OUR LOVE-*LESS* PAST

Beginning June 20, 2016, ten of the fourteen leaders of the Orthodox Christians met for their first Holy and Great Council meeting in 1,229 years! This unity meeting has been on and off for fifty years. Ecumenical Patriarch Bartholomew of Istanbul, Turkey, has given twenty years directly to this project. But four Orthodox leaders, including Patriarch Kirill of the one hundred fifty million-strong Russian Orthodox Church, skip the meeting because they feel the preparation has been inadequate. Yet the Patriarchs who do gather hope that a meeting like this can possibly take place maybe once every ten years. I mean, who likes meetings anyway?

There is a serious issue at hand and it has many layers to it. Bartholomew is a uniter. He wants the Orthodox Church to strengthen their unity, but he also wants to heal the schism of the Orthodox and Catholic Church, a division that dates back a millennium. This would mean healing creedal divisions, as well as accepting the possibility that love should take the lead even when there is a serious doctrinal difference. There are centuries of real and perceived betrayals and accusations, wars and détentes, and an official commitment to status quo. Yes . . . *official*!

In 1757 the Ottoman Sultan Osman III responded to an attempted hostile takeover of the Holy Lands by the Greeks with an edict that called for permanent *status quo*. This resulted in six different Christian groups claiming the Church of the Holy Sepulchre, the holiest site in the Holy Lands. But the arrangement of status quo states that not one of them can make any change or update, including much needed upkeep or repairs, without the complete agreement of all the others *on every last detail*. This is why many of these holiest sites are in disrepair, and why there has been a ladder under a window on a balcony of the Church of the Holy Sepulchre for nearly three hundred years. Called the Immovable Ladder, it represents a paralyzed church.

Consider the irony. The world population is exploding. The environment is bullied by humanity. Elementary-aged girls are sold to adult men as sex slaves. Terrorism morphs like a super-virus. The military industrial complex grinds human lives into return on investments, and the prison industrial complex acts as a storage complex for humans. But the church can't even move a ladder! When love does not lead, the church loses its way.

No matter where you come out on the Orthodox Church or the Catholic Church, what do you see in Bartholomew's example? I was deeply convicted by Bartholomew's example of a love that endures all things. With forty-eight hours to go before the first unity meeting in more than a thousand years, Russian Patriarch Kirill, the most influential of all of his fellow Patriarchs, backed out.

What would you have done? I might have considered taking the Immovable Ladder down and thumping Kirill on the head with it! What did Bartholomew do? He continued with the meeting, made no disparaging remarks about Kirill, and said he hoped that within ten years they could make this thing happen.

Is the Problem Love or Doctrine?

The answer is yes, and yes. I do believe it is a problem with our orthodoxy.

Not all churches have formal creeds, but all are concerned with orthodoxy—with getting it right. These official and unofficial ways of stating what we believe give us a sense of unity and security in our faith. It feels as if we are part of the people who have rightly divided the word of truth. But what if we simply left out—failed to honor—the first and greatest teaching of all? The outcome of such an omission is publicly highlighted by the Great Schism, but it can be seen in every Christian tribe in the world.

Creedal Priorities

What we believe matters. Depending on your faith and your personal walk with God, your doctrinal priorities may be arranged differently than another believer's. This difference in how we prioritize doctrines can become as divisive as separate creeds.

An early adventure as a young believer taught me this hard lesson. I had joined some fellow college students on a summer mission trip. We were outside of Pittsburgh, meeting people in the neighborhood to tell them about a new church. A family invited me in and jumped headfirst into a conversation about my conversion. They wanted to know if I had been baptized and if I had received the Holy Spirit. I was excited since they were emphasizing two of my big priorities. "Yes, on both counts!" I reported with excitement.

But then they wanted to know if I spoke in tongues. Not only did the church I attended not speak in tongues, they taught that anyone who did was wrong. Clearly, we prioritized this doctrine differently. The conversation quickly deteriorated, because once they knew I was a non-tongue-speaker, they questioned my baptism and whether I had actually received the Holy Spirit. Their conclusion was "no" on both, and my conclusion was that I was in over my head.

I stammered around and asked if I could use their bathroom. I had heard people speak in tongues a few times when I visited other churches, but I quickly dismissed it because it wasn't *orthodox*—it wasn't *right according to my church*. What was I to do? I thought about staying in their bathroom and hoping they would forget I was in there, but I opened the door and headed back into the fray. When I entered the living room, they offered me a solution: "Why don't you come back Saturday morning? We called our pastor, and he will come and study with you, lay hands on you, and you will speak in tongues." "Okay . . . uh . . . yeah . . . that sounds good . . . see you Saturday." I kept a nervous smile on my face and feigned enthusiasm, but I was scared to death!

I wasn't going to tell any of the other students on my mission team what happened because we all came from the same kind of churches and I knew speaking in tongues was on their "no-go" list also. But I did call my fianceé , Susan (who's been my amazing wife and partner on this crazy journey for the past thirty-five years). She answered the phone, "Hey, Babe, how's it going?"

I stammered around, "Well, you know . . . today was pretty interesting."

"Oh, how so?"

Yikes! What was I going to say? Did I fail to mention that her dad was an elder in one of "our kind of churches." You know—the churches that believe tongue-speakers are faking it? I decided to go for it. "Saturday morning a pastor is laying hands on me, and I'm going to speak in tongues!" I blurted out.

Silence . . . "Hello . . . Hello, Susan . . . Are you still there?"

Her very first words were, "Don't tell *anyone*!"

She didn't have to warn me twice about the land mines of doctrinal prioritization. Just as some believers questioned my salvation because I didn't speak in tongues, our churches were teaching us to question the salvation of those who did. And I realized that most of my group thought it better for us to convert them or for us to just go our own way.

Does that last sentence haunt you a little bit? Before I tell you about my Saturday visit with the tongue-speakers, let's consider our doctrinal dilemma: Of all the doctrines we believe, prioritize, and defend, we do not believe love is on the list. Not literally. I know we believe in love, but we live by doctrine. Let's explore this a little further.

I have never met a Christian who was not able to quote verses that affirm that . . .

1. God is love.
2. God so loved the world that he sent his Son.
3. The greatest command is to love.
4. There is no greater love than to lay your life down for another.
5. The world will know we are Christians by our love for each other.

We know all of this. We can tell the stories, exegete the meaning, deliver the sermons, and write the blogs. Our bumper stickers remind the world to Love God and Love People. But if you've been around Christians any length of time, you may have noticed that we also split churches, mock ministries, and blast other believers. The darkest chapters in the story of the Christian religion are filled with us killing each other, enslaving each other, and abusing each other. There was no cruelty inflicted on other religions and foreign people worse than those we have perpetrated on fellow Christians.

That last sentence strikes a nerve. At our core, we struggle around the question, "If people believe in Jesus differently than we do, are they *even Christians at all*?" This question may be rooted in pride, insecurity, or a sincere desire to be faithful to the teachings of Scripture. But it gets horribly unnerving when we see videos online of ISIS soldiers beheading men, women, and children because they are "Christians." At that point, it seems unthinkable to ask, "What kind of Christian are the victims, or how do their doctrinal statements match up with mine?"

So we find ourselves somewhere between the reality that people are dying for the faith we share, and then trying to figure out what it means for us to hold firmly to what we believe to be the truth of God's Word. What role does love play in regard to pure doctrine? Can the Love-First creed be restored? Will we continue to be a love-deprived creedal culture, trading Christ-conditioned unity rooted in divine love for worldly disunity, mirroring the Satan-imitating, self-promotion of the world?

Will We Become the New Humanity?

In Ephesians 3:10–11, we read the true intentions of God for the scope of the gospel. The apostle Paul claims that the work to which he has been called is nothing less than the eternal purpose of God. "His intent was that now, through the church, the manifold wisdom of God should be made known to the rulers and authorities in the heavenly realms, according to his eternal purpose that he accomplished in Christ Jesus our Lord."

What is this "manifold wisdom of God" that is being proclaimed through the church to the rulers and authorities in the heavenly realms? In the previous chapter Paul explains:

> But now in Christ Jesus you who once were far away have been brought near by the blood of Christ. For he himself is our peace, who has made the two groups one and has destroyed the barrier, the dividing wall of hostility, by setting aside in his flesh the law with its commands and regulations. *His purpose was to create in himself one new humanity* out of the two, thus making peace, and in one body to reconcile both of them to

> God through the cross, by which he put to death their hostility. (2:13–16, emphasis mine)

Why did all this happen? What drove the heart of God to relentlessly pursue this audacious plan of redemption, reconciliation, peace, and abundance for all humanity? According to Paul, "*Because of his great love for us*, God, who is rich in mercy, made us alive with Christ even when we were dead in transgressions—it is by grace you have been saved" (Eph. 2:4–5). His eternal plan is rooted in his eternal love. That is why the psalmist exclaims over and over, "His love endures forever!" (136). It doesn't just last a long time; his love endures whatever it takes to create the new humanity wherein the culture of Christ-conditioned love can reign.

By the way, I did go back for the Saturday tongue-speaking study. We spent over six hours studying the Scriptures together. I didn't end up receiving the gift of tongues, and I later learned from Paul's first letter to the Corinthians that not everyone does. Our time together did not end in a circle, holding hands and singing "*I Love You with the Love of the Lord*." Actually, I left haunted by their concern that I was not a true Christian. But I also knew that most of my friends at the time looked on them with similar suspicion.

But I did receive a gift that day. I was forced by the situation to decide what kind of person I would be when inevitable disagreements arise in the body of Christ. These brothers and sisters were not intellectually dishonest, and they clearly loved God. They were concerned for me and wanted me to experience the faith that was important to them. Wasn't this what took me to their neighborhood in the first place? We understood Scripture differently, and that forced me to do more than study spiritual gifts; this forced me to learn how to love other believers who see Scripture differently. That experience taught me the most important witness for Christ was not my biblical intelligence, but my willingness to be a conduit for his enduring love.

Love First Reflections

- What has been your personal experience when it comes to the church's most glaring blunders in the past: a problem of love or a problem of doctrine?

- Read Ephesians 3:10–11. Who does God intend for his wisdom to be displayed through?

- What is it about Christ-conditional love that it endures forever?

- Write a prayer of thanks to the Lord in similar form to Psalm 136, with the alternating phrase, "Your love endures forever."

LOVE NEVER DISAPPEARS

I was in Hipsterville, better known as the Minneapolis-St. Paul International Airport. Only Silicon Valley could have a greater concentration of skinny jeans and iPads. I was waiting in a crowd of frequent flyers, all pretending to be nonchalant while stealthily positioning ourselves for the mad crush through the Sky Priority lane. Above my shirt pocket was our church logo, "LOVE**FIRST.**"

This guy next to me, who had to be from West Hipsterville (my hometown of Portland, Oregon), would not quit staring at my chest. More than a little awkward! Finally, he blurted out, "So, is Love-**First** some kind of hippy commune?"

I thought, "Well, it doesn't read Love**FEST**!" But I replied, "No . . . it's like . . . uh . . . umm," and I found myself stumbling. So what is LOVE**FIRST**? Especially in the world of everyday words where religious assumptions may not be in play? Finally, I unemotionally stated my real answer: "It's how I believe I should live." "Huh," he replied as he slyly slid past me in the Sky Priority lane. "That's cool."

LOVE**FIRST**. It *is* the logo on my shirt and the summary statement for what our church is all about, but in Hipsterville I discovered my core belief: loving others before I do anything else with them, for them, or to them *is how I want to live.*

Our world is fractured because we keep getting things out of order. We judge first, condemn first, yell first, whine first, post expletive-laced rants first, demean first, call people names first, bully first, spread lies and suspicion first, shoot first, blame and bomb first. It's all out of order. Jesus tells us to love first, and his followers have given their lives to make sure this Christ-conditioned gift to the world never disappears.

But do you feel loved by God? Have you worked it out in your own experience that God is love and God loves you? This is where it gets tricky in a hurry. If you don't feel loved by God, you may be wondering what in the world one of you, or both of you, are really up to. Have you screwed up so much that you question whether or not God has grown cool to the idea of loving you? Or have you suffered such pain that you have cooled to the idea of loving him, or trusting that he really is love?

You don't need to read another book to figure out that life is brutal when you don't feel loved. Nor do you need me to make a case that "everyone needs love." You already know these things. But throughout my thirty-plus years as a pastor, counselor, teacher, neighbor, father, and husband, nearly everyone I have met is struggling to fully experience love from others and from God.

The Embrace You've Longed for All Your Life

Everyone loves Julie. Parents, brothers, friends, husband, kids, and even our dog! I met her family when she was fourteen, but it wasn't until I moved with my family to Atlanta to serve as the preaching minister for our church that I reconnected with her story. I officiated their wedding when Steve and Julie married, and then some years later she became my assistant. My wife and Julie became fast friends, and our families have grown close over the years. Julie is immersed in love.

But there was a love she longed to experience. I will call it "first love." Different than how we normally think about our "first love," Julie wasn't thinking about her first boyfriend. She was thinking about her birth parents. Adoptions in the early '70s were often "closed," with no information shared or available. Her quest for connection with her birth parents wasn't driven by an absence of love. The Wilson family *is* Julie's family. She has known an abundance of love from the moment she was cradled in their arms for the first time. But like many who have been adopted, she wanted some answers.

Through decades of gentle prodding and fervent prayer, coupled with some online investigative skills, she found them. Her birth father had passed away, but her birth mother was still alive. Emails were exchanged. A meeting was set.

They met at a park in her hometown and her mind recorded every "first." The first sight. The first sound. The first touch. The first embrace. The first hug could have lasted forever. The first three hours were nowhere near enough. They had just met but there were tears upon parting, and their breaking away from their embrace felt like a muscle being torn.

Julie's birth mom gave honest, tender answers to her many questions. The Internet had yielded some dates. From their wedding date to her birth seemed like enough time to be conceived into their brand new family. "Was I the reason you got married, and then for some reason you didn't want a child?" This question gets to her deeper question, "Was I loved?"

"You were conceived in love," her mom answered. This was the "first love" that quietly and persistently drove her search for years. There is something about "first love" that matters, and how you came to your family is not necessarily what drives us to seek it. First love is the most pure and innocent form of love. It's that love that doesn't need to prove itself, be earned, or even known.

It's that take-it-for-granted kind of love when someone says, "Well, you know I've always loved you, and I always will."

First love doesn't wonder about looks, body shape, academics, or athletics. First love precedes and supersedes all that. And for that reason, we desperately seek it. Life is so out of control, so unfair. It has so many ways to trip us up, tear us down, and rip out our hearts. There are millions of Julies, adopted or not, who, yet surrounded by love, want the answer to one question: "Am I worth your love—just the way I am?" First love answers that question.

Being birthed in love matters, whichever way it went for you. If your heart aches when you read Julie's story, it might be that you, too, want to know. But it might also mean that you do know—that someone has growled at you that you were "the biggest mistake they ever made." Before I move on, I want to say that if you're enduring that kind of pain right now, I am sorry. I hurt for you, and I wish I had a magic wand that would wave it all away. But you, as much as anyone reading this book, understand what Julie was looking for, and why it was so important to hear her birth mother's words.

I Wish I Could Replicate Freddie Mae

We have felt the sting of someone taking advantage of our vulnerabilities, or dropping condescending disses when we miss the mark.

My friend John's mother passed away. I rarely take notes at a funeral, but this one was the exception. Freddie Mae Stroop's son started by stating, "Her life was love." Then her daughter caught my attention: "Mom was a pure expression of compassion and love. She was surprised if others did not respond to her with the same generosity of spirit she showed them." The preacher noted, "Freddie Mae had no trouble believing that everyone is born in the image of God and therefore is worthy of being loved. I wish I could replicate Ms. Freddie Mae."

The world can feel demanding, dehumanizing, and dangerous. People are plagued by isolation, even when they are in families, crowds, sororities, or churches. We listen and look for signs of acceptance, but we know the "ties that bind" are thin these days. One thing is clear: we didn't need Facebook to get unfriended. But then along comes a Freddie Mae with a heart overflowing with Christ-conditioned love, and it changes how we experience our lives. Freddie Mae determined that her love for others would not disappear even if their love for her never did appear.

Not All Circumstances Are Equal, but Love Is Love

Susan and I have always been surrounded by amazing marriage mentors. Sometimes these couples are younger, but mostly they have been in their autumn years, calling us deeper into the love Christ modeled for us. One couple has had such an impact on our lives that I am not sure where they leave off and where we began. Their marriage is the first I ever described as "epic."

I will start off with the uncomfortable stuff! They were known for "public" romance, sloppy kisses, and displays of affection that were thinly veiled as "oops" moments. Their personal love notes to each other would make John Legend hang up his career. This was their storied life.

And for the last fourteen years, as this sweet wife, mother, and grandmother stepped ever farther into the thickening mist of Alzheimer's, well . . . only the tears running down my cheeks as I write this can capture the respect that floods my heart. This mentor of mine seems never to tire of the repetition familiar to all who've stumbled down this path, nor does he lose the gleam in his eye for her when the tantrums and tirades often associated with this disease spew forth from the sweetest voice his ears have known for nearly sixty years. And when the tempest quickly goes out with the tide of forgetfulness, she cuddles in his tender arms, safely, securely, surely loved. *This is the love that never disappears.* Mother Teresa gently chastises us, "Love, to be real, must cost, it must hurt, it must empty us of self."

The Trajectory of Love

For love to never disappear, it must be on a path that insures growth. That trajectory is not easy, but it is simple:

> More love . . . less hate.
> More courage . . . less fear.
> More humility . . . less arrogance.
> More empathy . . . less selfishness.

Henry Drummond places the emphasis on our transformation into the character of Christ. To the degree that we share in his likeness, is the degree that the conditions of his love will be experienced through us. "God is love. Therefore love. Without distinction, without calculation, without procrastination, love. To become Christ-like is the only thing in the whole world worth caring for, the thing before which every ambition of man is folly and all lower achievement is vain."[1]

The way of love is not a transaction that improves our chances of getting what we want from someone else. The signature love of the church is not simply an occasional burst of compassion in response to crisis, but rather we are a culture of never-disappearing love, always protecting, always believing, always hoping, and always enduring.

You Were the Tiger and I Was Pi

One Sunday evening in 2013, our adopted son Jerome spent an unforgettable evening with Susan and me. Through our son, Aaron, we had met Jerome when he was a young teenager. Aaron and Jerome were the same age. Through a series of events too complex to recount here, Jerome came to live with us during high school. Over time we all sensed that God had in mind something very special, and we became a "forever family." The judge who presided at the adoption asked our other children how they felt about Jerome becoming their brother. To that, our youngest son, Caleb, replied, "He already is my brother."

Jerome had been through a lot. Things he saw and experienced are not fit for an adult, let alone for a vulnerable child. Sometimes, like this particular evening, Jerome would open up a part of his life and share some of his inner feelings and thoughts. I will never forget what he shared. He said, "When I first came to live with you, it was like the movie, *The Life of Pi*. I was the boy, and you were the tiger in the boat. I didn't know if I could trust you, but I knew I needed you. When I was a little boy, I prayed for a dad, I prayed for a mom, and I prayed for a family."

As the evening continued, tears flowed. Why does any little boy, or girl, anywhere in the world ever have to search and pray and cry out for a family to love him or her? Why does anyone, anywhere, who is within the touch of a follower of Christ have to look twice, listen twice, or think twice about whether or not this person will be safe and love them. No server at a restaurant, no nurse in a hospital, no teller at your bank, no student in your school, no player on your team, and no person in your church should ever spend a day wondering if love has disappeared from the earth. Our love should be recognizably distinct—Christ-conditioned—offering a generous welcome into patience, kindness, and the "always" culture of divine love.

The Corinthians' Conditions

Gen Ed courses are the curse of Western education. Many a salutatorian has a Gen Ed professor to thank for their second-place finish. Personally, my GPA was trampled under the militant march of a professor who believed that Art 101 would be *the* difference between a future of stocking shelves or fulfilling my God-ordained destiny on planet Earth. The final exam was Exhibit A for this assault on my academic record. "You will have one hour to name, date, and classify one hundred images from art history, including the sculptor, artist, or architect. Ready? Proceed."

I clicked on the first image and stared at the screen. "Hmmm. Okay . . . come back to this one." Click. "Uh . . . is this one upside down?" Click. "Okay . . . looks like an ink blot . . . "Then the self-talk began . . . "Don't panic, Don. There is nothing wrong with stocking groceries for Piggly Wiggly!" Click. Then it happened. I came to an image I recognized! "That's a Corinthian column!" The students around me jumped at my outburst of excitement. "Sorry," I whispered, and with the confidence of a five-year-old that has just nailed the alphabet for the first time, I marked "Corinthian, Doric, and Ionic." Got 'em all!

Twenty-five years after my hard-earned B- in Art 101, I visited the Archaeological Museum of Epidaurus in Greece. Modern archeologists found and displayed the capital of a Corinthian column carefully buried in the foundations of a circular *tholos*. It puzzled researchers, but the most widely accepted explanation is that it was the sculptor's model for the stonemasons to follow. The tholos was normally in the center of town, a place in the market where goods were sold and official weights and measures were kept. The sculptor created a model by which all the rest of the columns would be shaped and measured.

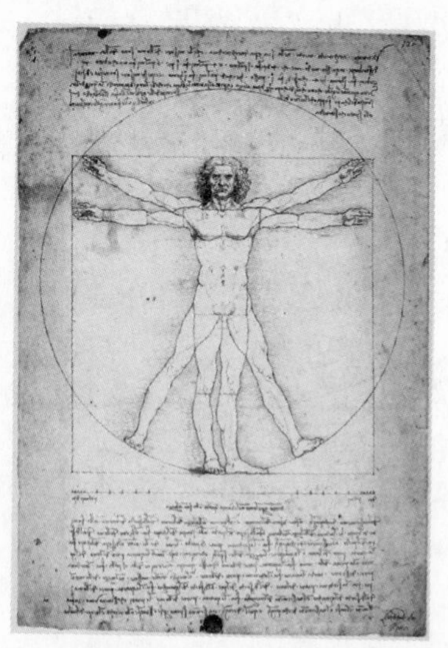

Another image from Art 101 is important here: *Vitruvian Man*. You may not remember Vitruvius, but you know his timeless image made famous by Leonardo da Vinci. If you have small children, Morgan Freeman was the voice for the character Vitruvius in the 2014 Lego Movie. Who is this ancient Greek who makes his way into a da Vinci and then stars in a movie two thousand years after his death?

Vitruvius lived around the time of Jesus and is the most influential architect in history. His *De architectura* was dedicated to Emperor Augustus and is the only surviving major book on architecture from classical antiquity. His work inspired generations of artists, thinkers, and architects. Vitruvius is famous for asserting in his book that a structure must exhibit the three qualities of *firmitas*, *utilitas*, and *venustas*—that is, it must be solid, useful, and beautiful. Architects have "orders," or uniform established proportions, regulated by the office that each part has to perform. In other words, there are strict *conditions* in architecture that must be met for the structure to be solid, useful, and beautiful.

Each style of ancient architecture is distinguished by its proportions, characteristics, and details, and this is what makes them readily recognizable. The sculptors and stonemasons had to meet the conditions of each architectural order that a building or design required. With his writings and influence, Vitruvius raised the Corinthian column to rank in the first century BC, codifying the design for all time. We recognize the Corinthian column because the design conditions set it apart from other forms. My grade on the test reflected my ability to know the difference.

Vitruvius wasn't the only guy writing in the first century about construction and building codes. In his first letter to the Corinthians, Paul describes himself as a *sophos architecton*, popularly translated "wise masterbuilder." But you don't have to know Greek to see "architect" in this verse.

> Or, to put it another way, you are God's house. Using the gift God gave me as a good *architect*, I designed blueprints; Apollos is putting up the walls. Let each carpenter who comes on the job take care to build on the foundation! Remember, there is only one foundation,

> the one already laid: Jesus Christ. Take particular care in picking out your building materials. Eventually there is going to be an inspection. If you use cheap or inferior materials, you'll be found out. The inspection will be thorough and rigorous. You won't get by with a thing. If your work passes inspection, fine; if it doesn't, your part of the building will be torn out and started over. But *you* won't be torn out; you'll survive—but just barely. (1 Cor. 3:9–15 THE MESSAGE, emphasis mine)

Paul is not in a restoration project with the Corinthians, simply trying to clean up the mess. Rather, he is in a rebuilding process where he has to tear down what was not built correctly and replace it with the proportions and measurements that meet the conditions of the owner of the house.

Like a building inspector who knows the house isn't safe, Paul walks them through, room by room, pointing out where they've cut corners. Now their living conditions are not safe. This is the problem with "unconditioned" living. It's not safe. This is why Vitruvius gave criteria beyond how something looked. It had to be solid and useful as well as beautiful to meet code.

The Corinthians needed a ground-up rebuild, but what is it that actually went wrong? Bad mortar? Termites in the wood? Paul describes the problem as "bad material," but what made it bad? It turns out it was counterfeit. All the problems in Corinth are rooted in one destructive decision: they had abandoned *Christ-conditioned* love. They chose to love as they defined it rather than to love as God designed it. Paul is going to drag them back through the long list of their own problems until they are sick of their sickness. Then in 1 Corinthians 12:31 he is going to propose that there is a way out of this mess, but it is the way of love—*the most excellent way.*

Chapter 13 in the first Corinthian letter gives us the conditions we must follow to love as God loves, so that we can live as God wants us to live. Now we must live those divine standards—the conditional love of God that is recognizable, like a Corinthian Column, the love which by design looks like the Designer.

Love-First Reflections

- Have you "worked it out in your own experience with God—that He is love, and that he loves you"? Is there an experience that stands out when God's love showed up for you in a personal way? Write down your thoughts.

- Who in your life has best modeled the Christ-conditioned standard of love?

- "Love to be real, must cost, it must hurt, it must empty us of self" (Mother Teresa). How does the world respond to this kind of real love?

- Like a Corinthian column is recognizable because of its design, how does living a Love-First life help the world recognize Jesus in you, and in your church?

- Write 1 Corinthians 13:4–7 in your journal, or on a 3x5 card, posting it where you can frequently meditate over the Love-First conditions.

- Choose four people with whom you will practice the conditions of divine love.

  One from work or school ____________________________
  One from your family _______________________________
  One from your church ______________________________
  One from your neighborhood __________________________

  Write down what it is about them that could make loving them a challenge.

  Write down what it is about them that makes you want to love them the Love-First way.

  Write down how you will begin to show them the love you are learning from this study.

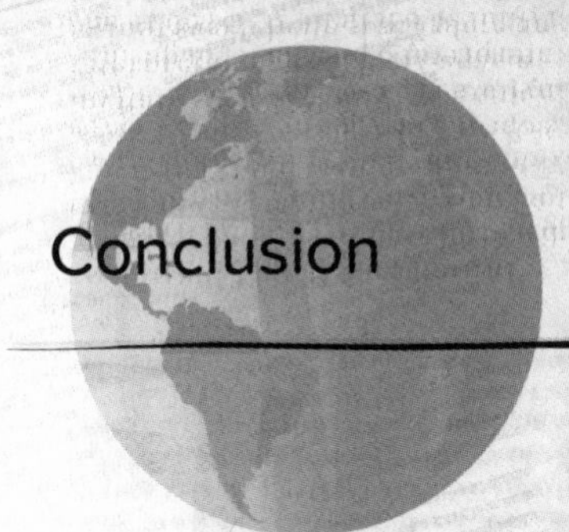

Conclusion

ONE THING REMAINS

"If you do not love first, you often will not get the opportunity to love second."—Ken Snell

Jesus calls us to love first. There is no sensible way to deny the crisis we face. It is not in the world; it is in *us*. The church, which is the body of Christ, is God's solution, but the world sees us as the problem. The reason for this is much deeper than just bad behavior. The only hope of the church to rise up to the full potential of God's vision for the new humanity is to humble ourselves again before him and ask the Holy Spirit to fit us with a willing heart to submit to the conditions that make divine love distinct. This will create a cross-culture that draws all to the matchless love of God displayed through Jesus. This is what Love-First is all about. But now what?

You will have many choices from all we have studied together. You will have much to consider, talk about, wonder about, and perhaps debate about. I believe that Christians who live by the Love-First Christ-creed will shape the future of their communities and change the course of history. So I hope you will consider one parting challenge: Love-First is a way of living, not just the logo on my shirt.

What would it take to launch the Love-First Movement? What would it take for this description of love to be the most natural praise of our hearts, but also the most-often-cited characteristics of our lives? What would it take for you to launch a Love-First community movement in your school, at work, in your neighborhood, in and through your church?

When I reflect on my journey with God's Love-First gospel, I am taken back to an early experience where I witnessed a church begin a transformation of love at the close of the shortest sermon in history. Our church was friendly and welcoming, caring and compassionate, but I knew our love was shallow. We sang about it, prayed about it, and studied about it. But when the inevitable challenges of doing life together got under our skin, tempers would fly, rumors would multiply, and hate would do its dirty work among us. Finally, one Sunday morning I got up in the pulpit and began this way: "Please turn in your Bibles to John 14:15 and read along with me . . ."

We read together: "If you love me, keep my commands."

"Now, please follow along with me in John 14:23."

We read, "Jesus replied, 'Anyone who loves me will obey my teaching.'"

"And finally," I coaxed my people, "please read with me John 13:34–35."

Together we read, "A new command I give you: Love one another. As I have loved you, so you must love one another. By this everyone will know that you are my disciples, if you love one another."

"So," I exhorted my church, "love one another." And then I sat down.

That was the entire sermon. Go ahead and read through it right now and time yourself. Did it take you about forty seconds? That's about what it took me that morning.

Well, the church started squirming. Wasn't I going to preach? What in the world was going on? So everyone just sat there.

I got up a second time, preached my forty-seconds-long sermon again, emphasizing "love one another," and then sat down.

Once again . . . nothing but fidgeting, whispering, and murmuring.

So for a third time (come on, this is *not* a complicated lesson!) I got back up and preached the same message.

But this time when I sat down, one of our younger men got up, went over to another person, and began to talk, show concern, and love on them. Soon it was another person, and then another.

Within about five or six minutes, the church was filled with the sounds of obedience to the commands of Jesus: Love had broken out! And it wasn't just any kind of love. It was Love-First. It was the kind of love that superseded all of our conventions, codes, and unwritten creeds. It was the love of Jesus that rises high above everything else. In fact, there was really only one accurate description after the service: "Of all that we did today, *the greatest of these was love.*" As I wrote this study for you, I prayed that God would work in you and through you.

- I pray that love is breaking out in your life.
- I pray that your vision of love has been transformed.
- I pray that the Love-First creed of Christ has captured your allegiance.
- I pray that your love is so conditioned by the Spirit of Christ that others cannot help but know that you love because he first loved you!

- I pray that in every arena of your influence, you will Love First and help the world end hate before it's too late.

Let me encourage you with Paul's prayer in Ephesians 3:16–19 (NLT):

> I pray that from his glorious, unlimited resources he will empower you with inner strength through his Spirit. Then Christ will make his home in your hearts as you trust in him. Your roots will grow down into God's love and keep you strong. And may you have the power to understand, as all God's people should, how wide, how long, how high, and how deep his love is. May you experience the love of Christ, though it is too great to understand fully. Then you will be made complete with all the fullness of life and power that comes from God.

ENDNOTES

Introduction

[1]In the case of sensitive and confidential stories, the names have been changed.

Chapter 1

[1]Bryan Loritts, "Luke 19 and the Segregation of the Church," *The Exchange: A Blog by Ed Stetzer* (January 20, 2015), accessed January 27, 2017, http://www.christianitytoday.com/edstetzer/2015/january/luke-19-and-segregation-of-church.html/.

[2]Hillary Ferguson, "The Ugly In Christianity," *Huffington Post* (June 8, 2016), accessed January 27, 2017, http://www.huffingtonpost.com/entry/the-ugly-in-christianity_us_57588f08e4b053e219786f6b/.

[3]Roger Olson, *The Mosaic of Christian Belief: Twenty Centuries of Unity and Diversity*, 2nd ed. (Downers Grove, IL: InterVarsity Press, 2016), 24.

Chapter 2

[1]Pope Francis, "Chrism Mass Homily" (March 28, 2013), accessed on January 27, 2017, http://w2.vatican.va/content/francesco/en/homilies/2013/documents/papa-francesco_20130328_messa-crismale.html/.

Chapter 3

[1]Philip Jenkins, *The Lost History of Christianity: The Thousand-Year Golden Age of the Church in the Middle East, Africa, and Asia—and How It Died* (New York: HarperOne, 2008), 146–47.

Chapter 4

[1]C. S. Lewis, *The Weight of Glory* (1965; repr. Grand Rapids: Eerdmans, 1973), 15.

Chapter 8

[1]Jerry Morgan, *The Change Moment: Finding that Critical Moment in Time When You Are Changed for All Time* (Abilene, TX: Leafwood Publishers, 2012), 92.

Chapter 9

[1]Henry Drummond "The Greatest Thing in the World," accessed February 17, 2017, http://www.ccel.org/d/drummond/greatest/cache/greatest.pdf/.

[2]I am indebted to my Tuesday morning men's Bible study group for their insights on kindness.

Chapter 10

[1]John Short, "1 Corinthians," *Interpreter's Bible*, vol. 10 (Nashville, TN: Abingdon Press, 1953), 175.

[2]Ibid.

Chapter 12

[1]Robert Putnam and David Campbell, *American Grace: How Religion Divides and Unites Us* (New York: Simon and Schuster, 2010), 103.

[2]*Global Gospel: An Introduction to Christianity on Five Continents* (Grand Rapids: Baker Academic, 2015).

[3]"Why are Christians so rude?" Accessed February 16, 2017, http://www.topix.com/forum/city/ashland-ky/TSEMAHHQ3K2GDSSPU.

Chapter 13

[1]This quote is an adaptation of C. S. Lewis's words from *Mere Christianity*, Chapter 7 (San Franscico, HarperCollins). It was first adapted by Jud Wilhite in *UnChristian*:. *What a New Generation Really Thinks About Christianity* (Grand Rapids MI: Baker Books, 2007), 198.

[2]John Nolland, *Word Bible Commentary: Luke 9:21–18:34*, vol. 35b (Dallas: Word Publishers, 1991), 592.

[3]Ibid.

[4]Ibid.

Chapter 14

[1]Corrie Cutrer, "The Silent Epidemic," accessed February 17, 2017, http://www.todayschristianwoman.com/articles/2004/september/silent-epidemic.html/. Sojourners; "IMAWorldHealth and Sojourners—Broken Silence: A Call for Churches to Speak Out," accessed on February 17, 2017, http://www.imaworldhealth.org/images/stories/technical-publications/PastorsSurveyReport_final.pdf/; Bob Smietana, "Pastors Seldom Preach About Domestic Violence," LifeWay Research, June 6, 2014, accessed on February 20, 2017, http://lifewayresearch.com/2014/06/27/pastors-seldom-preach-about-domestic-violence/.

[2]World Health Organization, "16 Days of Activism Against Gender Violence," accessed February 17, 2017, http://www.who.int/violence_injury_prevention/violence/global_campaign/16_days/.

[3]Brant Hansen, *Unoffendable: How Just One Change Can Make All of Life Better* (Nashville: W Publishing Group, an Imprint of Thomas Nelson, 2015), 6.

[4]Hitendra Wadhwa, "*The Wrath of a Great Leader: Martin Luther King Junior*" (January 21, 2013), accessed November 9, 2016, http://www.humintell.com/2015/01/the-wrath-of-a-great-leader-martin-luther-king-junior/.

Chapter 15

[1]Corrie ten Boom, *The Hiding Place* (1971) quoted in Bryan Lowe, "The Hiding Place– Corrie ten Boom Learns to Forgive," Brokenbelievers.

com, accessed February 20, 2017, https://brokenbelievers.com/2016/02/05/the-school-of-forgiving-corrie-ten-boom/.

[2]Martin Luther King, Jr. "Love and Forgiveness," Delivered to the American Baptist Convention (Atlantic City, NJ, May 5, 1964) pp. 3, 5–6, accessed February 17, 2017, http://www.thekingcenter.org/archive/document/love-and-forgiveness/.

[3]Ibid.

Chapter 16

[1]Deuteronomy 32:4; 1 Kings 10:9; Micah 6:8; Amos 5:14–15, 24; Isaiah 42:1–4; Matthew 12:17–20; Psalm 33:5; Psalm 99:1–4; Hosea 12:6; Zechariah 7:9.

Chapter 17

[1]David Mathis, "Let's Revise the Popular Phrase, 'In But Not Of,'" DesiringGod.org, accessed February 18, 2017, http://www.desiringgod.org/articles/let-s-revise-the-popular-phrase-in-but-not-of/.

[2]Gabe Lyons, "What Does Being Countercultural Look Like?" Accesssed February 17, 2017, http://qideas.org/articles/what-does-being-countercultural-look-like/.

[3]Ibid.

[4]Ken Snell, personal discussion with the author, North Atlanta Church of Christ, 2016.

[5]Lesslie Newbigin, *The Open Secret* (Grand Rapids, MI: Eerdmans, 1995).

[6]"Human trafficking brutal and widespread in Georgia," CBS 46 WGCL-TV report, accessed February 17, 2017, http://www.cbs46.com/story/24425994/human-trafficking-brutal-and-widespread-in-georgia/.

Chapter 19

[1]Karen Franklin, "The best predictor of future behavior is. . . . past behavior," *Psychology Today* (January 3, 2013), accessed February 16, 2017, https://www.psychologytoday.com/blog/witness/201301/the-best-predictor-future-behavior-is-past-behavior/.

Chapter 21

[1]Dallas Willard, *Renovation of the Heart* (Carol Steam, IL: Tyndale House, 2002), 131–132.

Chapter 24

[1]Henry Drummond "The Greatest Thing in the World," accessed February 17, 2017, http://www.ccel.org/d/drummond/greatest/cache/greatest.pdf/.